JUNIOR COLLEGE DISTRICT

of St. Louis — St. Louis County

LIBRARY

7508 Forsyth Blvd.

St. Louis, Missouri   63105

PRINTED IN U.S.A.

Model Making

in Paper, Cardboard and Metal

Model Making

in Paper, Cardboard and Metal

George Aspden

Photographs by Derek Abbott

Reinhold Publishing Corporation
New York

© George Aspden 1964
Printed in 12 on 13 pt Modern No. 1
Published in Great Britain by Studio Vista Limited
Published in the United States of America 1965
by Reinhold Publishing Corporation
Library of Congress Catalog Card Number 64–25856
Printed by Staples Printers Limited, Rochester, Kent

Printed in England

Contents

List of Plates

It is not what the teacher does for the pupil, but what the pupil does for himself that matters. SOCRATES

INTRODUCTION
a collection of themes and variations

This book is addressed to all people interested in model making. They may include the amateur in any age group who makes models for pleasure; the teacher or instructor in craftwork; people involved in exhibition or display work; and countless others who are simply interested in making things.

The idea for such a volume developed originally from an educational necessity amongst a group of teachers. With little previous experience they found themselves wanting to do model making with their pupils, approaching the subject creatively.

Beginning with the idea that artistic solutions can never be taught, but only the craft relating to a subject, one solution to the problem was to devise various basic forms suggesting bird, fish, animal and human. These were to act as a point of departure for experiment. Experiment and free interpretation are the keynotes of this particular type of work.

Together with the diagrams on how to begin making the shapes, this book includes suggestions for alternative effects. The illustrations indicate such possibilities, and they may be copied wholly or in part. However, their chief function is to act as a stimulant. The models shown are all of manageable table-top proportions. The more ambitious works can be enlarged and adapted as display units.

It is hoped that interested readers will derive much that is of practical value from this storehouse of ideas, and that it will encourage them to more ambitious efforts. If the book can lay claim to this achievement then its purpose will have been justified.

7

MATERIALS

The basic materials are grouped below. It is only necessary to select one item from the paints listed, and a choice of adhesives is also possible, though it is recommended that all those listed should be available for use when required.

MATERIALS	TOOLS	ADHESIVES	PAINTS
paper	pencil	gumstrip (self-	poster colours
cardboard	ruler	adhering	designers' colours
perforated zinc	scissors	paper tape)	metallic paints
wire	pliers	brass fasteners	enamel
		seccotine (or	
		white emulsion	
		glues)	
		fine wire	

paper

All the paper models illustrated were made with a good-quality cartridge paper which was thick enough to withstand constant handling, folding and cutting. Some of the pieces which were stuck on to the models as accessories were of thinner cartridge paper, and in one or two instances sheets from a writing pad were used. Paper as a medium for model making is too universally known and understood for further comment here. It is full of virtues within its limitations. Remember that it has one justifiable tantrum. It can behave quite peevishly when correct measurements are slighted or ignored. Try to stick paper into positions for which it has been incorrectly measured, and it will tear itself in half rather than obey.

cardboard

Thick cardboard, and the thicker the better, but not so thick as to make working laborious, has the quality of greater permanence than paper. It stays in position without wilting and does not tear easily. When used as a panel fastened with gumstrip to wire frames, it comes into its own

PLATE 1

PLATE 2

PLATE 3

PLATE 4

as the perfect material for this particular type of work. It is not necessary to buy special sheets of cardboard. All the models illustrated were made from ordinary packing cases. Shoe boxes and sweet boxes were used when finer card was required. Some strawboard (common pulp cardboard) was used, but this tends to flop and sag when painted. These sheets should be given a coating of thin glue 'size' before being made up into models. Gummed on both sides and laid out flat to dry they become quite tough.

perforated zinc

This is a perfect material for model making, and it forms the basis for all the metal models illustrated. It is very pleasant to handle and is obedient when manipulated. It will twist and curve into any position and stay put, though if it is bent flat against itself it is liable to crack. Two gauges of this material which can be cut with large household scissors have been used: thirty gauge and twenty-six gauge. Finer gauges can be used when making models on a miniature scale. When bought from the shop this metal invariably looks tarnished and unattractive in appearance, but clean it with household metal polish and you will give it a mirror-like surface. After a few days, however, this surface will tarnish and become dull once more, so it is advisable to paint the model with enamel or metallic paint. This acts as a preservative as well as giving a decorative effect. As this material is expensive in quantity, it is advisable to cut every shape from a paper pattern which has first been tried in position on a wire frame. This eliminates a lot of waste.

wire

Three gauges of wire were used for the models. This is the florist's type of wire which has no resilience and keeps the angle at which it is bent. The strongest is sixteen gauge, black annealed wire. It is used chiefly for the framework of the models, on to which are stuck or wired panels of card or metal. The medium strength is eighteen gauge, black annealed wire. This can be called the modelling wire. It is used for shaping hands, birds' feet, etc., and for special edgings to metal shapes, and is, in fact, a 'jack of all trades'. The finest wire is fuse wire, or radio-spares wire. This does all the binding and tying together of the frame as well as holding the metal panels and accessories in position. Other suitable gauges may be used according to what is available, but steel springing wire should not be entertained.

scissors

Two types of scissors are necessary: the ordinary small household scissors used for cutting string and paper, and a large heavy type, often referred to as 'shears', which are tough enough to cut the sheets of perforated zinc.

pliers

There is usually a bewildering variety of pliers displayed in hardware shops, but most of them are designed for a specific purpose. Any pair of pliers which will bend wire to make a small complete loop is suitable; if it also includes edges for cutting the wire it is the tool we are looking for. The rosary pliers of German make are ideal but they are not widely sold by stores. Second-best to these are small round-nosed pliers to make loops, and a jewellers' snip or shear for cutting wire.

gumstrip (self-adhering paper tape)

Throughout the book there is hardly a paper or cardboard model which has not a tab of gumstrip sticking on it some-where. It is used extensively on all the cardboard models because of its one crowning virtue, immediacy. It sticks fast at once. There is no question of holding the model pressed between finger and thumb, waiting for it to dry, as with other adhesives. It is possible that a model may end up looking like a brown patchwork quilt when finished, but

14

a coat of paint will obliterate this effect. All the cardboard shapes are stuck to the wire frames with gumstrip only. Cellophane tape is not advisable because it will not take colour and is less pleasant to work with in other ways.

brass fasteners

These two-pronged fasteners are another inexpensive product that have the same property as the gumstrip. They are used for joining paper shapes together, and are the perfect medium for holding the straps of the paper masks. The medium-size fasteners are the most useful.

seccotine (or white emulsion glues)

These adhesives stick the extra pieces on to paper and cardboard models. In this capacity they have a hundred and one uses.

fine wire

This is the general term for wire which is used chiefly as a binding agent. Fuse wire and radio-spares wire, which have already been mentioned, are ideal for the job. If the models are very much enlarged from their prescribed proportions, then soldering would be a more practical proposition. There is no special rule for binding two pieces of wire together, or for tying a panel to a frame. Use the wire as if it were a strong piece of thread, and when actually binding two shapes together pull the wire as tight as possible.

poster colours

For the paper and cardboard models, poster colours are the ideal paint to use. They are cheap and economical in large quantities. If new stocks have to be bought, make sure there are double quantities of black and white. These can be mixed with other colours to create an opaque effect, which is necessary when painting the surface of the cardboard. It is advisable to give the models two or three undercoats of a chosen colour, which allows the other bright colours to make their full impact. On paper models these opaque colours look more effective than tints.

designers' colours

These colours are manufactured to have greater degrees of brilliance than the poster colours. They are also more expensive. One or two of the colours will not stand over-painting as they tend to bleed through any superimposed colour. Some are also liable to fade quickly when exposed to a bright light. Otherwise, the information concerning poster colours applies equally to designers' colours.

metallic paints

There is quite a wide range of metallic paints in the trade catalogues, including red, green, bronze and copper. The two most popular colours are silver and gold. There is usually only one silver paint listed, and this presents no problem. With gold, there is often a choice of four shades, but the most suitable is the one known as green gold. There are several reasons for this. If gold and silver are to be combined on one model, this is the colour which looks best. It also looks good in isolation, whereas the other shades, when viewed in certain lights, tend to appear slightly tarnished. And it is a good mixer when placed against most self-coloured backgrounds.

enamel

The range of enamel colours is enormous. If there is no specific colour scheme in mind, it would be worth considering the dramatic quality of an all-black model when given a red setting, contrasted with the light airiness of a model painted all white.

USE OF MATERIALS

Metal graters, garden labels, curtain rings, metal and bone buttons, are some of the objects absorbed into the basic shapes of these models. One is sometimes tempted to pile a large quantity of such objects on to a single model. But when this happens the finished result is not the blended effect of a face, bird, fish, etc., but an untranslated collection of bric-à-brac clinging to and encrusting a wire frame. The reader must understand the meaning of the word 'translation' as used in this context. The brother of 'translation' is 'transformation', which means a complete change from one shape to another. It is impossible for the materials to make this change. What they can and must do when a number of them are thoughtfully placed together, is combine to create a total effect far greater than their separate selves; they become translated. Colour acts as a unifying agent, and one colour used on a model made with a variety of materials is able to subdue the clamour for attention of numerous bits and pieces, and thus produce a completely harmonious effect. All artists and designers worthy of the name know that ideas are more important than the materials which help to realize them. Materials must always be the servants, never the masters; the idea always comes first. In all fairness, however, it must be stated that unless we play around with our materials – selecting, matching, rejecting, accepting, trying out unusual combinations of materials – the good ideas will not come.

DECORATION

Decoration for paper and cardboard models will consist chiefly of painted details, though plain work with only a single colour may be preferred; much will depend on how the model is developed. Usually colour and decoration imply one and the same thing, but here they are discussed separately.

When painting, realize from the start that, even if the model cannot be viewed entirely in the round, there will be a front, two sides and possibly a top or base view to be linked together with some unifying effect. This is very important.

To create any effect at all requires a build-up of details. If the model is based on a living creature, its own attractive markings may be used to advantage, though modifications will be inevitable. However, not every creature has been endowed by nature with distinctive effects of colour and design, even though its outline may be attractive. Dragons and other beasts which cannot be drawn from life rely entirely on illustration sources and the imagination of the modeller. When such a situation occurs, the following suggestion is offered. Study the creature modelled and take special notice of the various pieces used in its construction. Some of these may be quite simple and attractive in themselves. Choose one or two of these shapes and repeat them enlarged or reduced as painted decoration. This approach makes it easier to avoid an unrelated and confused effect.

Spots and stripes are the simplest form of decorative repetition. Variations on the spot-and-stripe theme are endless and their popularity is universal. They may be used just as effectively on bird, beast, fish or human.

It would be a mistake to attempt to paint realistically such things as fur or feathers on this type of model, for the effect would be incongruous. A practical alternative to painted shapes is artificially created textures – such as coarse sawdust – or fine corrugated paper which could be used to advantage if applied in small quantities and with discrimination. These materials must also be painted.

A thoughtless use of decoration can destroy the scale of a model and this happens when indiscriminate, fussy or exaggerated pattern smothers the surface and demands attention. On a well decorated piece of work all the separate details are unobtrusive and work together to make one united effect. When you are ready to decorate the model it is helpful to work out any special details on paper first. By doing this, various possibilities may be explored. It is preferable to decorate the models after they are constructed rather than paint the paper or cardboard before assembly. If work is done this way the details may not look so finely executed, but the general effect will be more spontaneous.

When you become doubtful or undecided about decoration and feel that the model itself does not really provide a lead it is wise to use shapes and patterns of a chiefly geometric nature. Nearly all the models here reflect this quality in their basic construction. If you always work towards obtaining a finished product which has variety, balance, harmony and restraint, and if the general effect looks convincing, then the final result cannot be criticized for being overloaded, fragmentary, unbalanced or monotonous.

COLOUR

Colour plays a very important part in this type of model making. When used successfully it appears to be indispensable to the shapes it decorates. To understand its proper use better we must remember that however attractive the colour scheme may be, it cannot improve the basic quality of a model; it cannot make up for any structural weaknesses in a design. The model itself, with its natural high-lights and shadows (however slight they may be), is of primary importance. Colour stands by, waiting to embellish. When brought into action it is used to enrich the surfaces in order to make the artist's idea more compelling.

It is easier to show a person where he has gone wrong with colour than to instruct him on how to go right. Rules and regulations for colour schemes often produce mediocre results when put into practice, and equally, totally successful schemes have come from an apparent breaking or ignoring of rules. It is the placing together of large and small quantities of colour side by side and at angles, and the unexpected influence they exert on each other, which produces the most surprising and successful results. Keeping these remarks in mind and considering the model (which already has built-in effects of light and dark) the method of procedure is clear. A scheme needs to be worked out which matches a colour to each individual shape, unless the model was planned originally with a particular colour scheme in mind.

Either decorative or naturalistic colour can be used, but it is as well to remember that the natural colouring of some tropical creatures could well rival the most decorative scheme that could be invented by an artist. If the model resembles a certain type of creature and the effect is convincing the right impression will remain whatever colours are decided on.

Some artists work with a very small number of colours and do not find this a hindrance. Others require a whole range of colours to achieve their effects. A limited palette is usually a blessing in disguise, and the beginner would be

PLATE 5

PLATE 6

well advised to consider no more than three or four colours as the maximum quantity for any model. Even enlarged models stand to gain in effectiveness by this restriction.

A very good model may create its own colour scheme. This is best explained by saying that when it is finished, it is difficult to think of it being painted with any but a certain colour, or set of colours. When this happens an artist feels suddenly confident about everything he does, and this is the best way to work. Unfortunately, this ideal way is the exception rather than the rule.

It will be appreciated then that colour is largely a matter of individual preference and experience, and the following remarks are offered merely as a pointer.

Red and green placed together complement each other. So also do yellow and purple, and orange and blue. These three groups are often used as the basis for colour schemes, and any original starkness of effect generally becomes modified as the scheme evolves.

One warm and two cold colours usually work well in combination; or one cold and two warm colours. A scheme of unrelieved cold colours (purple, blue, green) tends to look depressing. An arrangement of secondary colours (orange, green, purple) all of the same tone, looks drab but may be enlivened by introducing a primary colour (red, yellow, blue). A medium or light toned colour placed on a black background becomes luminous while darker colours become enriched.

In practice these specimen rules usually hold good, but sooner or later the modeller resorts to the more absorbing method of trial and error to obtain most of his best results.

SOURCES OR REFERENCE

Unfortunately, not everyone lives near a zoo, an aquarium or a museum. Such places, and those rare theatrical productions which make use of bizarre and compelling costumes and masks, are ideal sources of stimulus for the model maker. They quicken his imagination and make him realize that the range of possibilities for all subjects is inexhaustible.

Even so there is no reason to be discouraged. There are other sources of inspiration and, if left to ourselves, there is enough of the actor in all of us to fashion a mask with some sort of individual expression, however slight. We are also all well enough acquainted with birds and fishes to know that their variety is infinite, so that nothing we could make is likely to seem too fantastic to be real, provided that the parts of our model are sensibly related. The more enterprising amateur will manage quite ably without reference to other sources, and produce interesting results. They may look homespun when compared with more professional work, but they will be his own work and he can take some pride in his achievement.

When we really do require outside help, then illustrated books are the great standby. Animal and nature books, illustrated encyclopedias, and books on the history of costume are all obvious choices. And on inquiry, a librarian may supply specialist books indirectly connected with the subject which may be of the utmost value. For example, an artist wishing to study horses may leaf through various books of painting and photographs, before he suddenly finds what he wants – a book on oriental pottery illustrating clay statuettes of horses.

Books which deal with the arts and crafts of the primitive peoples of the world help in a way that few other books can. After a first quick glance the modeller may reject a lot of the examples as being too alien for his taste, but later, when he has grown accustomed to them, their value and usefulness will become apparent. From such sources can be learnt the art of making much out of little.

The African native carves realistic and symbolic masks

and statues from wood; these range in effect from crude and simple forms to works which display an amazing elegance and refinement. The islanders of the South Seas have produced masks, carvings and painted decoration of startling originality. Ancient Mexico gives us stone carvings of figures, animals, masks and gods, and a great variety of pottery vessels usually shaped with animal or human forms. Moreover, their hand-weaving has patterns and borders with a strong geometric flavour in which bright earth colours are featured. The art of the American Indian, from the plains and deserts to the north-west coast, provides a rich treasury of superb designs: totem poles; masks; carved utensils incorporating animal, bird and human shapes; weaving; ceremonial costumes; all are objects which will repay keen study. Eskimo art, though it has a more limited range of subjects, can supply us with ingeniously designed masks.

The literate cultures of the ancient world, such as Egypt, India and China, provide another rewarding field of study. Their range of artistic creations is infinitely more varied and far more subtle and civilized than that of primitive peoples.

These ancient and modern primitive peoples living close to nature and the supernatural world of magic have provided the modeller with designs and objects which can furnish him with practically all the stimulus he needs, once he has overcome any personal prejudices and can approach their creations with an open mind.

Before the Industrial Revolution made itself widely felt in Europe and America, furniture, household utensils, costumes and church furnishings were lovingly decorated by people living in country districts, who found this work an outlet for self-expression. Their products are usually classified as peasant art, folk art or popular art. A distinct range of motifs was used, with birds, human figures and plant forms predominating as subject matter on a wide variety of objects. An eagle could just as easily decorate a plate, feature in a piece of embroidery, be carved on a bed-head, be used as a repeat for hand-loom weaving, be shaped into a gingerbread mould, or painted on a linen chest. Such a widespread use of one particular motif may seem very restricting but with each new article to be decorated a fresh interpretation would be envisaged. At its best folk art has great individuality born of personal ingenuity; really large collections are housed in national museums, and there are also good illustrated books on the subject.

Ideas may come from a variety of sources and at the most unexpected times, but not all of them may be worth developing to the model stage. Occasionally an idea may happen by chance. For example, the head of a strange animal may gaze out from the shapes of a certain type of joiner's vice, though only one person can see it; or a few blobs of ink pressed between a folded piece of paper may suggest a head with collar and crown. These associated ideas can be useful as a starting point, but once the modelling has begun the object or shape which first inspired the artist must be discarded completely; his own idea now grows and develops from it. The finished animal face must carry no suggestion of a joiner's vice, and in the mask we make there must not be the slightest indication of an accidental ink blot. Such ideas have their value when they catch the eye and make a great impression, but if anyone deliberately searches for similar effects he will find himself trying to force ideas from very unwilling material; and this must be avoided at all costs.

GENERAL REMARKS

To obviate disappointment, construct the first model according to specification. Then experiment afterwards with the second and third model.

Be thorough in all your working, whether making the simplest or the most complex models.

Construct the metal and cardboard models as though they were intended to last for ever. There is nothing more frustrating than a rickety structure.

When handling pieces of wire and metal expect to collect a quota of small scratches. These are inevitable and easily dealt with by a dab of antiseptic. Wires and bits of metal often catch on woollen clothing, but most of these snags are eliminated with practice.

Cardboard models may be painted with oil colours, and masks made with strong cardboard are the perfect vehicle for this medium. Before starting to paint give the model a liberal coating of cold glue 'size' which must be allowed to dry out completely to make a hard surface. Cover this surface with an oil primer, and when it is dry the preparations are complete. Oil paint is a very tractable medium. It takes longer to dry than other paints and, if corrections have to be made, details can be rubbed out, scraped off, or even painted over while in a drying state. Turpentine cleans brushes, palette and hands.

Consider wood as a fourth material to paper, cardboard and metal – nothing grander than ordinary kindling wood and balsa. They could easily be absorbed into this type of model making.

It has been noticed that even a small group of children or adults who start off being merely interested, and then become absorbed by the job in hand, invariably produce unexpected results of marked individuality.

Never be wholly discouraged when a very ambitious experiment turns out a flop. Some of the greatest failures may engender some of the greatest successes.

Models

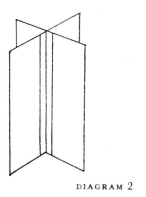

DIAGRAM 1

DIAGRAM 2

DIAGRAM 3

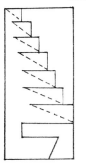

A FOLDED ONE-PIECE MODEL

PLATE 2

For this model a single piece of cartridge paper is required. The paper can be of any length and width, but the suggested proportions for a try-out are 9 *in* by 12 *in*.

Fold the paper into four equal widths, each 3 *in* by 9 *in*. Press together the two middle sections, and fold the two outside flaps at right angles to them. Stick with a length of gumstrip to seal the folds in position as in diagram 1. The result is a three-winged bracket which stands very firm.

The two flaps held with gumstrip form a large surface on which to paint a figure. The folded support behind the figure should be painted a dark colour and have its top corner cut away to be less conspicuous.

An alternative is a four-winged construction. Fold and stick the paper as above, slit the fold of the middle section and ease the wings into position. The length of gumstrip will hold this arrangement quite firmly (diagram 2).

If strong paper or thin card is used these two models will withstand a lot of handling. They are more satisfactory than the commoner four-winged model made of two panels slotted into each other, for the wings are less liable to swivel together.

comments on plate 2

The tall figure standing in the centre of the page is a three-winged construction. If required, the silhouette could be asymmetrical. The candle, the pollarded tree and the four perching birds on a tree, the star and the flower are all four-winged shapes. Each of the flower leaves is folded in half from leaf-tip to base. The house with figures is a four-winged shape with the base of each wing cut and folded into a triangle. A door shape, which can be turned into a figure, is cut in each wall.

The construction of the fir tree is shown in diagram 3. It consists of a series of diminishing rectangles cut one above the other with an allowance for the central trunk, each

29

rectangle being folded diagonally. This design looks particularly well when a forest of trees of various sizes is stuck on to a panel.

The front flap of the hen makes the head and chest only; the back flap forms the body and tail. Diagram 4 shows one of the two side flaps which are folded into wing and foot shapes.

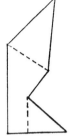

DIAGRAM 4

suggestions

Construct pendant shapes of flower or foliage to hang from a series of concentric hoops diminishing in size, in chandelier fashion. The spots in diagram 5 show the points of suspension for the shapes. If very large four-winged shapes are made with cardboard, it is advisable to make right-angled brackets of card to wedge horizontally between these wings as in diagram 6. On each of these four ledges place a small three- or four-winged shape to stand upright. Stick other shapes to point down from the underside of these ledges.

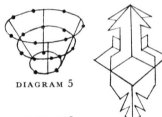

DIAGRAM 5

DIAGRAM 6

PLATE 7

PLATE 8

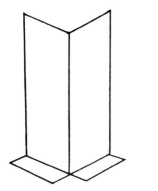

DIAGRAM 7

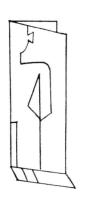

DIAGRAM 8

DIAGRAM 9

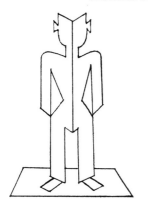

SINGLE-FOLD FIGURES

PLATE 3 (top row of figures)

One piece of strong paper or thin card, size 11 *in* by $7\frac{1}{2}$ *in*, forms the figure. A cardboard base is required, which could be a circle 4 *in* in diameter or a rectangle 6 *in* by 3 *in*.

Fold the piece of paper in half lengthways. From one end, measure a strip $1\frac{1}{2}$ *in* wide across the two halves. Score it with a knife. Bend this narrow strip outwards, and cut it in the middle to allow the paper to stand folded as in diagram 7.

Fold the paper flat and, using the full length of the folded edge, draw a very full half-figure shape as in diagram 8. This shape represents a man in the diagram, his feet being cut from the flap on the lower edge. Cut out this silhouette and cut away a narrow strip on the fold to divide the legs.

Fold him at a right angle and stick him with his two flaps on to a cardboard base, as in diagram 9. The top of his head is left flat to allow for a hat.

comments on plate 3 (top row of figures)

These figures are all folded at a right angle. The cowboy is wearing a hat, which is a single piece of paper slotted into a cut made on each side of the head. The fish girl, the peasant, and the official are also wearing hats made by this method – a method which causes the bases of the shapes to be hidden by the front of the head. By treating this space as a special detail, or adjusting the face to fit it, the hat and face can be blended together.

The cowboy also wears a circular holster and neckerchief. The fish girl has long arms which are folded forwards to hold a large fish across her apron. Notice that the space between the legs is not divided as with the cowboy; the ankles would be too weak to support the figure.

The peasant girl has very angular arms and shoulders which bring out her character. Notice that her feet are contained in the vertical fold and not fashioned from the ground flaps. The bird and the tree are separate pieces

33

wedged behind the thumbs. The eighteenth-century official has no separate pieces other than his hat, so play has been made with decorated surfaces.

suggestions

The subject matter for these figures can be taken from history, geography, literature or religion, and thus this is an ideal type of model for schools.

Make the bases effective by painting them in appropriate colours to resemble grass, pebbles, carpets, etc.

A further development is possible through the construction of a rectangular base. Along the back edge and sides of the base stick a three-sided screen of paper a few inches high, on which is painted a distant background. Use tabs of gumstrip to hold it. Do not include a sky area, but cut the top edges in silhouette. This little background helps to provide the figures with a stage-setting atmosphere.

Paint sunburned mountains and cacti for the cowboy; cobbles, baskets of fish, and ships' masts for the fish girl; gaily-painted peasant houses for the peasant; and a palace with railings and black-and-white tiled courtyard for the official.

CUBED FIGURES

PLATE 3 (bottom row of figures)

Two pieces of strong cartridge paper are required for this type of figure. In diagram 10, *A* is 12 *in* by 4 *in*, *B* is 12 *in* by $3\frac{1}{2}$ *in*. Both pieces are folded in half lengthways. *A* forms the front of the figure; using the full width of the paper, divide it lengthways, into four equal sections. Design your figure on this surface, remembering that parts of the two middle sections are to be cut away to show the background.

Take *B*, already folded, and rule a $\frac{1}{2}$-*in* margin on both the long edges. Score these lines and fold in reverse to the centre fold. Paint the inside of *B* before sticking to the back of *A*.

The diagram shows part of a back view of *B* stuck in position.

Sections of the $\frac{1}{2}$-*in* margins on each side of *B* may need to be cut away where they do not come into contact with the figure.

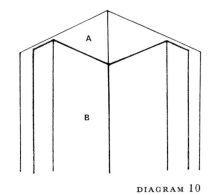

DIAGRAM 10

comments on plate 3 (bottom row of figures)

These figures, constructed on the principle of an elongated cube, require complete stylization. Except for the knight holding his sword, they are symmetrically designed and their effectiveness is achieved by an interplay of solids and voids. If they are to withstand rough usage, they should be stuck with tabs of gumstrip on to a cardboard base, 3 *in* square. Centre the figure on its base, angle to angle. With these figures, anatomical accuracy must be partly sacrificed to the desire for elongation. When painting, consider every detail, however insignificant, as a distinct shape with clear-cut edges, for the formal nature of the conception requires such treatment.

The woman with folded arms is a straightforward piece of construction requiring no special comment.

The knight is a largely symmetrical design with a displacement occurring in the centre area because of the arrangement of shield and sword. Note the simply arranged fingers and thumb holding the sword. The ankles are held firmly apart by retaining a narrow band of paper along the base line; the feet are extra pieces of paper. The back fold is cut as a pointed cloak and its line is carried through on to the front fold.

The mother and child differs from the straightforward cubed figure in only one respect: the two side flaps on B, originally turning outwards (see instructions) are reversed and stuck behind the crown.

The delegate from the East has foot shapes added.

All the figures will stand firmer with a base.

suggestions

The same subject sources as those recommended for the top line of figures would be applicable here. However, these figures tend more towards abstraction, being more decoratively conceived. By comparison the top line of figures could have a much more realistic interpretation.

PLATE 9

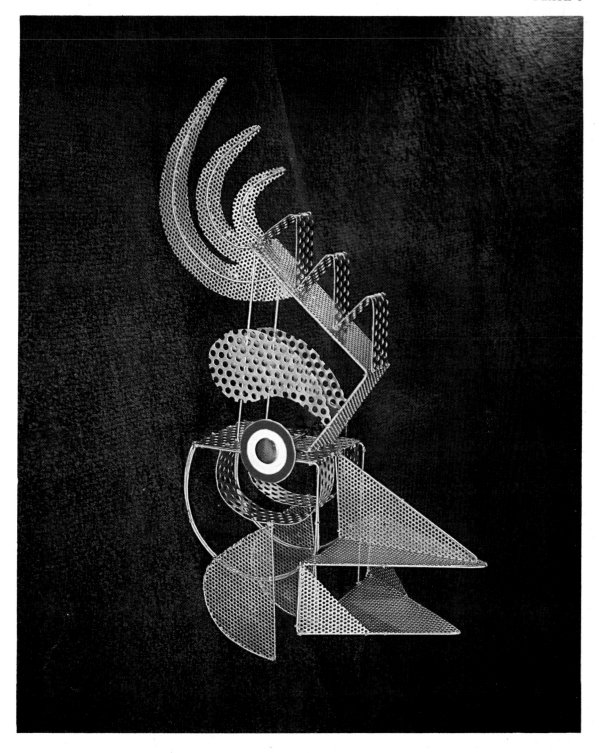

PLATE 10

PLATE 11

PLATE 12

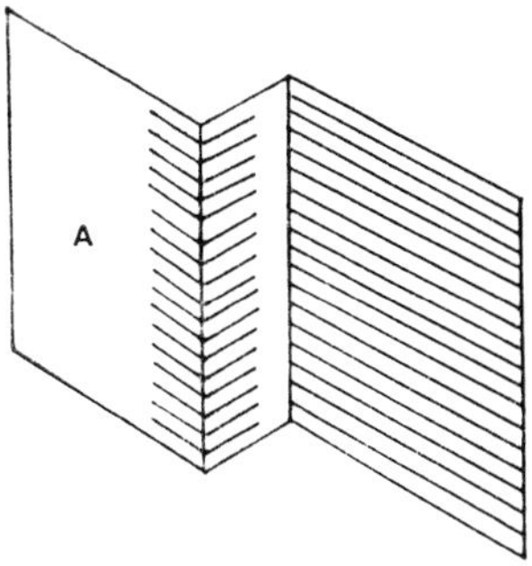

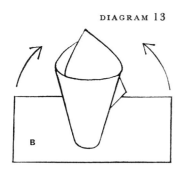

DIAGRAM 11

DIAGRAM 12

DIAGRAM 13

CYLINDER FIGURES

PLATE 1

For this model three pieces of paper are required. *A* is 15 *in* by 8 *in*, *B* is 5 *in* by 2 *in*, *C* is 12 *in* by 1 *in*.

A forms the body and neck. Divide it into lengths of 6 *in*, 1½ *in* and 1 *in*, leaving an end piece 6½ *in* wide.

Fold the paper on the 6-*in* measured line, and make cuts from this fold through the two thicknesses roughly ¼ *in* apart to the next measure line.

Take the 6½-*in* piece and fold the paper to point in the opposite direction. Cut it into long narrow strips (see diagram 11).

Roll the paper into a cylinder with a 1-*in* overlap. Fasten with brass fasteners or glue.

Tie the waist with thread.

Gather the strips for the neck and tie with thread, as shown in diagram 12.

B forms the head. Curl it into shape by pulling the two top corners together (diagram 13). Glue the broad overlap. Slide the head into position over the neck. Utilize the protruding strips for hair or headdress.

C forms the arms and hands and is threaded through the neck and wedged into two slits cut on each side of the chest, shown in diagram 14, p. 42. Any type of sleeve and hand shape may be cut from this strip, and the arms and hands may be folded to any angle.

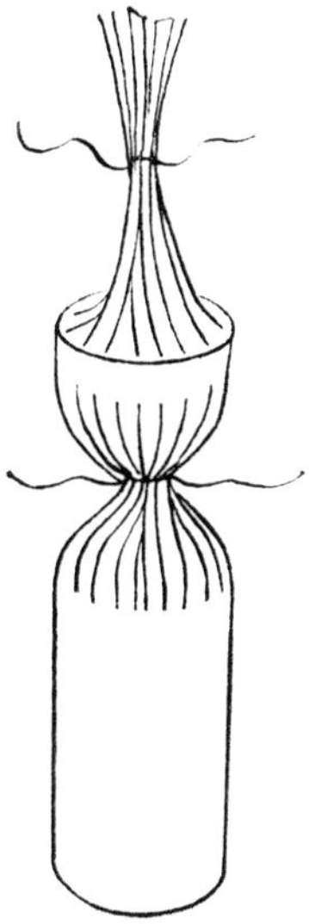

comments on plate 1

The negress has a dress composed entirely of border patterns of varying widths encircling the cylinder. This is an excellent idea for the decoration of a drum shape, for the variety of border patterns is endless and they always look effective. Notice also the variety of spots subtly echoing the idea of the top of a cylinder.

The queen of the night has parts of her design picked out in gold leaf. The turban is made by taking some of the long neck strips and bending them over to glue behind the head

41

piece. The remaining strips also looked effective when sticking up in a tuft of black spills before they were hidden inside the cone.

Both these figures were made from cartridge paper and painted after construction.

suggestions

If the figures are to withstand much handling it would be advisable to have a deeper and wider belt covering the wasp waist.

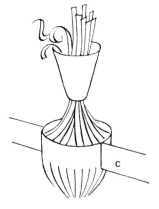

DIAGRAM 14

The figures illustrated are free-standing on their paper discs, but they could be stuck to cardboard bases cut in a variety of shapes.

By altering the angle of the arms and bending them forward, the figures can be made to hold objects suitable to their character. Short flaps or fringes encircling the lower half of the cylinder can be used effectively.

Bands of narrowly spaced matchsticks glued vertically to the cylinder look well when helped out with small discs of card, buttons or beads. A comparatively thin apron shape in paper, narrow at the top, wider at the base, and painted the same colour as the cylinder top, will suggest the end of a front sash. Slightly enlarged, it could be decorated and left as an apron.

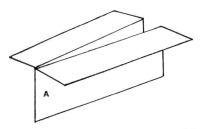

DIAGRAM 15

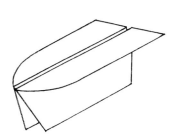

DIAGRAM 16

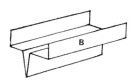

DIAGRAM 17

DIAGRAM 18

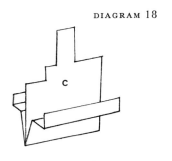

BOATS

PLATE 5

For this model two measured pieces of paper are required, plus other pieces to augment the basic structure. A is 11 *in* by $3\frac{1}{2}$ *in*, B is 5 *in* by $3\frac{1}{2}$ *in*.

A is the hull. Parallel to the long edges measure a strip $1\frac{1}{2}$ *in* wide. Score this line, and fold the paper in half across its length. Snip the fold to separate the two narrow strips, and bend them outwards as in diagram 15. These two flaps form the deck. Hold them together and cut them to a curved point as in diagram 16.

From both ends of the base line of the hull, measure 1 *in* and make diagonal folds up to the deck. Tuck in the fold at the prow. Overlap the folds at the stern to give a width of base, and glue them.

B is the measurement of the superstructure. Fold B in half across its length. On each side fold a 1-*in* strip followed by a second strip $\frac{3}{4}$ *in* wide. Fold these measurements as in diagram 17, and slot the shape in the deck.

C is the cut-out shape of a funnel, cabins, etc., which is slotted into B (diagram 18). Draw this shape to a suitable size and remember that an inch of it will be hidden below the deck resting on the groove of B. Add other details.

Compare this simple model with the possibilities shown in plate 5.

comments on plate 5

The oriental dragon boat has a hull 9 *in* long, and a deck $2\frac{1}{2}$ *in* wide. Each half of the long canopy is cut with spikes and long tail and a fringe of tassels. The spikes and tail on both pieces are stuck together, and the canopy bent into position; it is supported by six narrow strips of paper folded at right angles. The dragon head and neck is an extra shape stuck in position with a tab of gumstrip. The mast and the prow ornament are wedged in position.

The steamer has a hull $7\frac{1}{2}$ *in* long, and a deck 3 *in* wide. The centre of the deck is cut away, and the hull sides lowered and folded into side flaps. On to these is stuck a new piece of deck. The funnel is a tube of paper glued on to a paper box. The mast is a piece of card held in position with gumstrip.

The native craft has a hull 6 *in* long, and a deck $2\frac{1}{2}$ *in* wide. A short roof-top shape supports two triangular sails.

suggestions

To get the best effect with this boat construction, extra shapes and pieces need to be added. A brief glance at books on the history of sailing ships from all regions of the globe offers a collection of styles ranging from the mundane to the ultra-exotic, from the shabby one-funnelled tramp steamer to the glittering and resplendent Arabian Nights pleasure boat, decked out in peacock colours and flecked with silver and gold leaf. The three boats illustrated give the merest hint of how it is possible to ring the changes with the basic hull and deck proportions. All are made from cartridge paper. Sizeable craft can be constructed easily from cardboard. Models of this nature gain an added interest if a human figure is measured against them; and it is easy to supply small paper or cardboard figures cut to scale and stuck on to their bases with gumstrip.

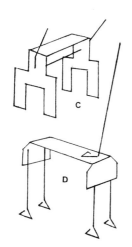

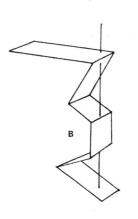

DIAGRAM 19

PAPER AND WIRE MODELS

PLATE 6

The models for this type of construction require no special measurements. The basic idea is to thread a long strip of paper, folded in square or rectangles, on to a length of wire. The small surfaces can be trimmed to any shape so long as they are not severed one from another. The wire supports the paper at any desired angle, and the folded effect of the paper gives bulk and mass. Shapes of cardboard may be incorporated in a design to hold wires in position, and to give contrast to the folded areas. All wires are stuck to the cardboard with gumstrip. If a human head or figure is attempted, vertical surfaces may be introduced and so change a simple construction into something more complex. The diagrams show skeletal frames of wire and cardboard for the designs illustrated.

In diagram 19

A shows two pieces of cardboard and wire rod for the beginnings of a head

B shows the build-up for the front of a head

C shows the cardboard frame and wire for a dog

D shows the cardboard frame and wires for a giraffe

E shows the wire rod and base with the construction for an African p. 34

F, *G* and *H* are the hat, face and beard shapes for a Chinaman.

comments on plate 6

The head, top centre, has a base and centre shaft of cardboard. The face and neck consist of one strip of folded paper. The nose is a triangle of paper which is folded in half and stuck so that it encloses the wire rod supporting the face. The eyes are made from the sloping plane behind the nose. From each side of this plane cut a length to hang free, and then fold it into shape. The mouth is an extra piece of paper. The back of the neck and hair are triangles and rectangles of paper.

45

For the dog, a length of cardboard has been cut into the shape of legs and a narrow spine. The body has large folds of paper trimmed at the lower corners. One end of the paper passes under the front legs to form the chest. Notice that the cardboard head echoes the chest shape.

The giraffe's body shape is similar to that of the dog. The paper is threaded on to the wires before they are stuck in position. The lengths of paper for neck, legs and tail are cut to taper almost to a point before being folded in diminishing lengths. The head is ten thicknesses of paper, cut and shaped. The two edges of the top piece fold upwards to make ears and eyes.

The African is made from a length of cardboard which is an equal width from head to foot, and is folded as in the diagram. The shoulders and arms are a separate piece stuck to the wire rod. Ears and nose are added shapes. The busby is a rabbit's tail.

The tree is a length of paper folded in diminishing lengths. Leaves and berries are added, and the wire trunk is slightly thickened with paper near the base.

The Chinaman has a centre rod of wire on a cardboard base. He has large folds of paper from the waist down, smaller folds from waist to shoulders, and smaller still from neck to head. The sleeves are diminishing folds threaded with pipe cleaners which are tied round the centre shaft. Diagrams *F*, *G* and *H* show the shapes for hat, face and beard. The wide collar slots round the neck, and paper hands have been stuck to the ends of the pipe cleaners.

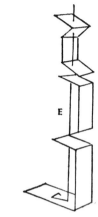

DIAGRAM 19

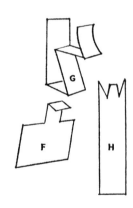

suggestions

As an alternative to sticking wires to cardboard frames when joining together the sections of a model, consider the following possibilities. Thread and twist wires round a large, medium or small size button before bending them to their final position; the joining of a body to the legs can be effected in this way. Use match-box cases without their trays, round cardboard pill boxes, or lengths of cardboard

46

tubing; these will all give a useful effect of bulk. Use small cartons and boxes as a basis for head shapes, and larger boxes for bodies; these may be painted with markings which carry on the folded paper effect.

Make a clown holding a wire hoop, with his collar and trouser top formed from shallow and wide-brimmed paper cones respectively, echoing his pointed hat. A round pill box or table-tennis ball could form his head.

Make a knight in armour, a spaceman and a magician. Make four-legged animals roughly based on real-life shapes, and other animals from imagination, taking your cue from the idea of the dragon. A dragon is the perfect subject for this type of modelling, with its arching neck, curling tail and body, and legs composed of a variety of widths and thicknesses.

The very simple head shape given in the illustration, is designed to show how a pleasant effect can be obtained with an economy of means. Using this basic construction, test your ingenuity with the help of all the various types of materials suggested throughout the pages of this book. Consider the following subjects: head of a warrior in fantastic gold and lacquered helmet with spikes and plumes; a creature from outer space; a woman with a bird hat; Neptune with a fish crown of blue-and-green metallic papers, and sequins in his beard; a noble savage with ceremonial headdress; a fantastic lady. Allow your imagination to have free expression within the scope of the materials used.

MASKS

paper, cardboard, metal

PLATES 4, 7, 8 AND 10

The construction of this kind of mask, with its basic face shape, gives the maximum effect with the minimum of effort. It scores over other methods because of its ease and speed of construction.

For a paper mask, one piece of paper $12\frac{1}{2}$ *in* by $10\frac{1}{2}$ *in* is required, and two brass fasteners.

Mark out the paper as in diagram 20. Cut away the two end pieces, and cut along the remaining lines to make seven loose flaps at each end.

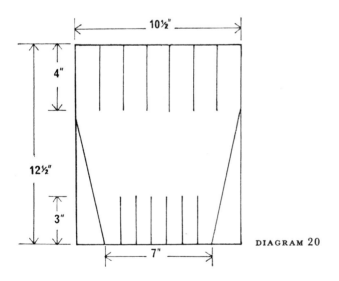

DIAGRAM 20

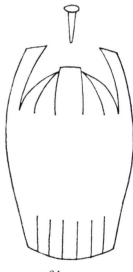

DIAGRAM 21

The large straps are pulled together to make the front of the head. Holding the centre strap, pull the other two pairs of straps underneath it on each side. Finally, overlap the two outside ones over all the others; pull them so that every strap is completely overlapping and secure them with a brass fastener. Repeat the same method exactly to form the chin. The closer the two sets of straps are pulled, the longer and narrower the face will become.

PLATE 13

PLATE 14

PLATE 15

PLATE 16

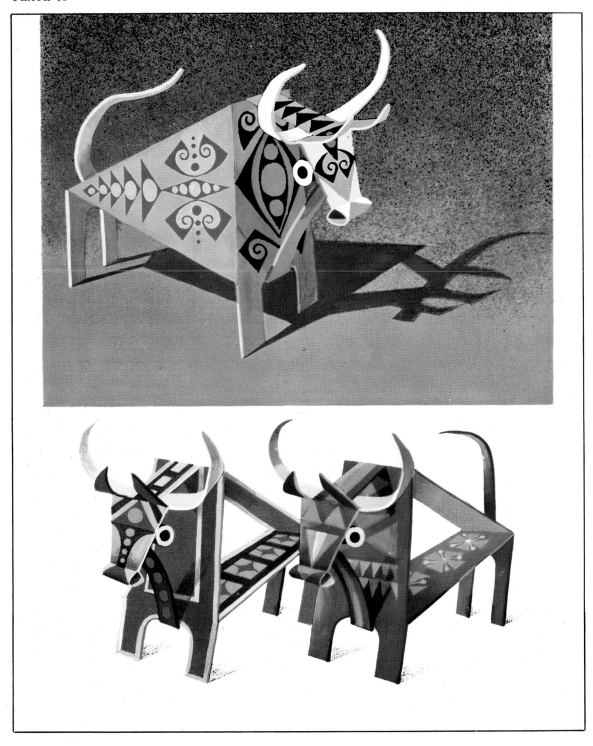

possibilities with masks

The mask shape offered here could be worn by a performer or could be used as a piece of decoration.

Two very different methods of designing a mask are worth consideration. One is to leave it bare of any added shapes, and to paint eyes, nose, mouth, hairline, etc., on the smooth round surface. The other is to use the mask as a foundation on which to build a complicated structure of facial details, which are painted very simply to allow the hollows and cast shadows to have a telling effect. Between these two extremes a vast range of effects is possible.

Mystery, strangeness and fantasy are essential if the mask is to achieve its maximum impact. If too much realism is attempted the finished effect will look dead and depressing.

subject matter

Remember that certain abstract ideas are ideally suited to personification: cheerfulness, sadness, calmness, ferocity, misery, famine, for example; or spring, summer, autumn, winter. The supernatural world of ghosts, demons, witches and magicians offers a wide scope. A more limiting range of subjects, inasmuch as each must vaguely suggest a character already depicted, is to be found in literature, opera, geography, religion, history and mythology.

some materials and their uses

When embarking on mask making, one becomes aware of the wide range of materials and bits and pieces of household stuff which, after a little doctoring and tailoring, may be absorbed effectively into a design.

Almost all the following materials would require the help of a little glue and paint.

hair and beards

Use wood shavings, brown paper, pipe cleaners, crêpe paper, bandage stiffened with wire and glue, raffia, drinking straws, paper and wood strips, horsehair, unravelled clothes lines, metallic papers, etc.

eyes

Use sequins, pieces of mirror, coloured glass, table-tennis balls cut in half, metal bottle tops, gold, silver, glass, bone and plastic buttons, large wooden beads, etc.

earrings and necklaces

These can be very satisfactory on masks. Use curtain rings, cardboard tubing, matchbox cases, bunches of small corks, melon seeds, tassels, etc.

headdresses

Use hen, turkey, goose and pheasant feathers, large beads wired or threaded on the ends of pipe cleaners, or thin cane, paper birds, fishes, fans and crowns, pieces of wired felt, etc. With decorative masks for panels, old straw hats cut in half and placed over the mask make an excellent foundation for added shapes.

surfaces

Cardboard masks may be covered entirely or partly with any lightweight material; sacking for a tramp mask is a good, if rather obvious, example. Fine or coarse net, chiffon, shapes of velvet, and striped or spotted material can be used ingeniously if applied with restraint. Other materials could include corrugated paper, bandages holding thick cord in position (for wrinkles), Christmas frost, coloured tissue and cellophane papers; use fur or rabbits' tails for eyebrows and moustaches.

comments on plate 7

From this group of seven masks, the nose, mouth and eyebrows of the warrior (top left) are made from additional pieces of paper. The nose is a three-sided pyramid, and the eyebrows and mouth are the halves of two wide elipses curved into position on the face. These pieces are held with tabs of gumstrip; all other details are painted.

The death's head (top right) is a painted surface only. The pupils are two large blue spangles which flash a cold, hard light.

The cuckold (centre left) has the concave sides of a table-tennis ball cut in half to make eye sockets, into each of which is stuck a wooden bead. The eyebrows are pipe cleaners. The mouth is two discs of superimposed cardboard glued into position.

The Chinaman (centre) has a folded triangle for a nose. A rectangle of paper is folded into a platform on which are painted the eyes. The mouth is a folded rectangle with a diamond shape cut in the centre.

The oriental (centre right) is a painted surface. The headdress is two loops of paper fastened at the temples. The top loop is folded into a point to give variety. The heavy-lidded eyes are circles divided exactly in half, the lower halves being painted darker.

The monkey man (bottom left) has a long folded triangle for a nose. Over this is stuck a smaller, wider triangle to form the nostrils. The tufts of fur are fringed paper wedged into the straps on the head.

The devil (bottom right) is a painted surface only. The horns are long curved triangles of paper wedged into the head straps.

All seven masks were made with strong cartridge paper.

comments on plates 4, 8 and 10

The exotic lady with the tall headdress (plate 8) was designed as a decorative panel. It was made entirely of cartridge paper but could easily have been made of stiff cardboard to be more durable. The mask was first stuck into position on the panel where it was to remain. Gumstrip was used for this. Extra pieces were then arranged on and around the mask to try out various combinations of effects. Loops of paper – two fringed along one edge and a third fringed along both edges to make a rosette, simple folded fans of paper and many folded triangles of paper are the only items which made up this elaborate decoration. The individual pieces are stuck separately on to the background, including the folded conical hat. The loops on each side of the head are tipped with glue and wedged under the straps.

55

The metal Indian lady (plate 4) is made from two masks. Number one is used for the face. Number two has the top of the head cut away, and is then turned upside down and wired into position on the head of the first mask, a high-domed crown being the result. On this crown is wired a row of garden labels, curtain rings, and metal buttons. Each curl of hair is a length of wire held by pincers and pulled into a coil. The eyes and mouth are buttons with a centre shape of metal paper. The nose is two triangular panels wired together.

The Silvanus mask in metal (plate 10) has a centre panel wired to the forehead, and is held in a backward slope by two wire angle brackets. The smaller waving crest is wired on to this centre panel. The two leaf shapes are held vertically with angle brackets. The hollow eyes are made by tying wire circles on to the mask and cutting away the eye space afterwards. This requires care and patience but the result is effective. The mouth is made in the same manner. Each strip of beard has a wire spine curled by twisting it into position.

suggestions

When large quantities of masks are required, a quick method of duplication is possible. Place the pattern on a small pile of sheets, and prick through with a compass point where all the lines begin and end. Then rule lines between these points before cutting.

When a decorative panel is used with a mask it should be remembered that this need not be restricted to a rectangle. Use diamond, oval, triangle and half-circle shapes. Consider modified versions of oak and holly leaf forms, but in each case ensure that the mask fits comfortably inside its boundary, unless it is placed near an edge to create a special effect. Whatever the shape of your panel (and however simple), use this shape as a decorative motif to be repeated ingeniously throughout your design. By doing this you will create a homogeneous effect, which is inherent in all successful pieces of design.

PLATE 17

PLATE 18

PLATE 19

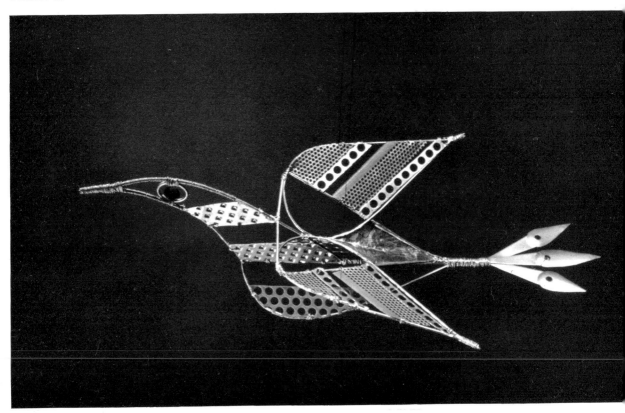

PLATE 20

Construct a totem of five masks on a long narrow panel. The centre mask should be of normal size; the ones above and below should have all their measurements reduced. Those at the top and bottom should be a few inches in height only, but large enough to show a pleasant gradation of scale.

Make two masks. Use the first one for the face. Cut the top of the head off the second an inch below the dividing straps, and fasten it upside down on the head of the first. Incorporate the upcurved effect in an elaborate hair style or headdress.

Construct a mask of black paper. Stick all over it a mosaic of very small coloured pieces of paper to suggest the features. To be effective each small piece of paper should have a very narrow margin of black background showing through. Help out the features with one or two brush strokes if they remain indistinct. To make the mosaic pieces cut up the coloured pages of magazines into very narrow strips and snip them into small squares. The basic mask measurements may be made half as big again to decorate a large room.

bird masks in cardboard and metal
PLATES 9 AND 11

The two cardboard bird masks are constructed in an identical manner. The golden cockerel mask in metal is a variation of the same theme. To make the cardboard birds, cut a box in half diagonally along its vertical sides, the box proportions being $4\frac{1}{2}$ *in* square and $3\frac{1}{2}$ *in* deep. One half of a box gives a complete head shape.

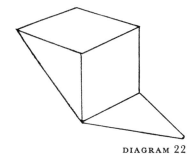

DIAGRAM 22

A triangular shape for the middle section of the beak is stuck with gumstrip to the lower edge of the box as in diagram 22. It is cut from a $4\frac{1}{2}$-*in* square of cardboard.

A triangular piece of cardboard forms the top of the beak. It is stuck in the centre of the forehead and stretches on its inclined edge from the top of the forehead to the tip of the beak. The eyes are sections of a cardboard tube.

DIAGRAM 23

A third triangular shape is cut for the lower half of the beak. This is $4\frac{1}{2}$ *in* wide and 4 *in* long. Its base is stuck to a wire frame as in diagram 23. Two small triangles cut from

59

a 2 *in* square of cardboard are stuck at the corners of the beak and against the wires. The projecting ends of the wires are then stuck inside the head with gumstrip, and the shape is complete.

comments on bird masks on plates 9 and 11

The bird mask in the top left corner has a strip of strong cardboard folded at a right angle and stuck to the back of the head and the inside of the beak. This strip is for holding the head in position when the mask is used as a wall decoration. The bird in the bottom right corner has two side loops of cardboard which function in the same manner. When decorating these birds, appropriate effects can be obtained by devising special shapes for combs and wattles. The top bird has a narrow rectangular box supporting a curved strip of card, on which is stuck a double fringe of paper; wattles can be made from flat boxes wired with a pipe cleaner, and paper tassels. The bottom bird has a paper fan-shape for a comb; the wattles are paper tassels stuck to sections of cardboard tubing, topped with a disc of cardboard and wired with a pipe cleaner.

The metal bird (plate 9) is constructed from meshes of perforated zinc tied to a wire frame which is built up as construction continues. In this model the forehead is left hollow and the eyes, which are metal buttons and discs of metallic paper, are wired to an axle passing under the top of the head. These three masks can be worn by performers if all the measurements are enlarged by 2 *in*.

suggestions

All types of large size, real feathers can be used effectively. Table-tennis balls can be used for eyes. Long raffia or paper fringes can be stuck along the entire length of the sloping sides of the head. A variety of circular crown shapes can replace the comb without destroying the bird-like illusion.

Make large wire loops to hang for wattles, and to these attach various pendent shapes of metal or cardboard; hang them both inside the loop and below it.

animal masks in cardboard

PLATE 11

The fiend face in the top right corner of plate 11 has a plat-form of cardboard $4\frac{1}{2}$ *in* by $5\frac{1}{2}$ *in* on which are grouped the eyes, ears and nose. Stuck at right angles to this shape are two side cheeks, cut with one curved edge and two straight edges of $5\frac{1}{2}$ *in* and $4\frac{1}{2}$ *in*. The two lower corners of the cheeks are held apart with a short length of wire. The mouth is a long strip of cardboard 8 *in* by 3 *in*. Fold one end into a step shape, and curve the remaining piece to form the lower jaw; then edge the two long sides of this piece with wire stuck with gumstrip to hold the mouth in position. Allow for two projecting lengths of wire at the top end which are bent and stuck under the face with gumstrip; this is the only attachment of the mouthpiece to the head. The nose, eyes, ears and teeth are pieces of cardboard. The side pieces are pipe cleaners sandwiched between lengths of gumstrip and cut to shape.

The dog face in the centre of the group has two platforms of cardboard held in position by the two cheeks, which are right-angle triangles with their pointed end meeting at the back of the head. These cardboard triangles have a 4-*in* base, and a vertical length of 6 *in*. The top platform is 8 *in* by $4\frac{1}{2}$ *in*. The back end of it is cut in a semicircle, which holds cardboard tubes for eyes and a folded card for the nose; a long strip of card is folded and trimmed for ears. The lower platform is held in position by two angles of wire running along the vertical edges of the cheeks and the horizontal edges of the jaw; on to this shape are stuck a cardboard tongue and teeth.

The cat face in the bottom left corner has a platform on which are stuck eyes, nose and ears made from a rectangle of cardboard 5 *in* by $5\frac{1}{2}$ *in*. One of the long sides has its corners cut away, leaving a narrow end 2 *in* wide with sloping sides $2\frac{1}{2}$ *in* long. A shape which is $3\frac{1}{2}$ *in* wide at the base, $1\frac{1}{2}$ *in* deep, and 2 *in* wide at the top is stuck to this narrow end to form the area above the mouth. The mouth is a box shape, whose two vertical sides measure $2\frac{1}{4}$ *in* by 3 *in*. The top and bottom of the mouth are two rectangles cut with sloping sides. One side is $5\frac{1}{2}$ *in* long, and its opposite $3\frac{1}{2}$ *in* long, the width between these two lengths being 2 *in*. Stick the four cardboard shapes together with gumstrip and join them to the flap at the front of the head as in the illustration. Fitting flush to the top of the head and sides of the mouth are two rear panels, 3 *in* by $4\frac{1}{2}$ *in*, which hold the face and mouth rigid. In the illustration they have been cut in half diagonally to allow the face to tilt forward when it is hung against a wall. Add pointed ears and a pointed chin of cardboard. Sections of cardboard tube form the eyes, and a narrow three-sided piece of card forms the nose. Whiskers may be cut from cardboard or paper or be made with bristles from a stiff brush. The curved tongue is attached to the back of the roof of the mouth.

suggestions

These three masks could be worn by actors if all the measurements were enlarged by 2 *in*.

Colour should be used decoratively when painting these masks in order to create a mood rather than a realistic effect, unless the mask is to be used for a performance where a specific colour is necessary.

The cardboard teeth of the fiend mask could be replaced by uneven stumps of wood, glued into position to give a sinister effect. Long strands of hair could be made to sprout from behind the ears and hang down the sides of the face. Coloured twigs could radiate from the top of the head.

Make the dog and cat from cardboard covered with silver or gold metallic papers. Various spot and stripe effects look well on these two creatures.

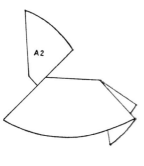

DIAGRAM 24

DIAGRAM 25

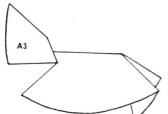

BIRDS

folded birds

PLATE 12

Two pieces of paper are required for the basic shape. *A* is 8 *in* by 5 *in*. *B* is 7 *in* by 4 *in*.

A is the body and is folded in half lengthways. From the folded edge draw a full curve as in the diagram, and cut out this shape. *B* is the neck and head; treat exactly as *A*.

From one end of the folded edge on *A* measure $2\frac{1}{2}$ *in* and fold over the corner. Tuck this flap inside. This recess takes the neck. With the paper still folded make a tail at the opposite end by cutting an inclined line almost to the folded edge. Fold this tailpiece upright as in *A*2. Then ease the tail backwards till it turns inside out – *A*3.

Take *B* already folded and cut to shape. Fold a flap at one end with its lower edge lying horizontal as in diagram *B*1 p. 46. Tuck this flap inside, as in *B*2. This is the head and beak. Cut away or fold some of the neck area to reveal more of the head. Trim the head shape. Stick *A* and *B* together.

comments on plate 12

The standing bird in the illustration is supported by a single piece of paper folded to make a front and two side walls. The side walls are cut with sloping edges. There are flaps at the top of these two walls holding the bird in position.

The flying bird has three additional pieces of paper – the comb stuck between the two sides of the head; the wings, which consist of a piece of paper pushed through a slit on each side of the body; and an elaborate tail. The tail is simply a long piece of paper folded in half, cut into a very detailed silhouette, and wedged into the body. The neck area is an unbroken curve folded back to form a collar. Knotted cotton, threaded from the inside of the head and the base of the tail, is tied together to make one strand for hanging. These birds were made from cartridge paper.

63

suggestions

It is possible to add an extra 2 *in* to all the measurements to enlarge this bird, but over enlarging would cause sagging and flopping.

To widen the scope of decoration make the bird in black or other dark coloured papers, and paint it with two bright colours. Cut feather shapes from metallic papers and use them on matt surfaces. Using this bird pattern as a guide, construct a similar shape in cardboard. Where the paper is folded add hinges of gumstrip. Inverted folds must be substituted with other ideas, but the main planes and their angles can be retained. Consider a similar construction to this with perforated zinc and wire as the chief materials.

cardboard birds

PLATE 14

Four pieces of cardboard are required. *A* is 14 *in* by $1\frac{1}{2}$ *in*, *B* is 7 *in* by 1 *in* and *C* and *D* are 4 *in* by $1\frac{1}{2}$ *in*.

A forms the body and tail pieces. Take *A* and make $\frac{3}{4}$-*in* cuts 1 *in* from each end. These cuts are made on opposite sides and slot into each other.

B is the head. Take *B* and make $\frac{1}{2}$-*in* cuts at both ends as in *A*. Slot together and stick to body.

C and *D* form the legs or base. Make $\frac{3}{4}$-*in* cuts in the centre of these pieces and slot them together. Stick them to the under side of the body, shown in diagram 28.

Diagram 29 shows the plan of a beak with eyes. When the beak is folded, the small tab between the eyes is glued to the front of the head.

Diagram 30 shows a construction for eyes. A small length of pipe cleaner has a cardboard disc at each end on to which a bead has been glued.

comments on plate 14

The panels used as fillings for head, bodies and bases are made by laying the model flat and drawing round the required shape. Cut out the shapes, glue liberally inside the

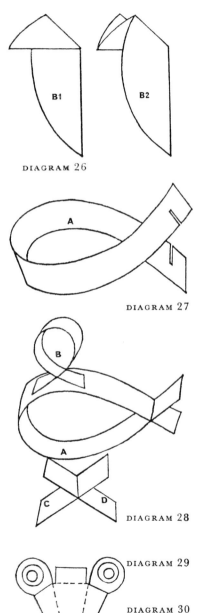

DIAGRAM 26

DIAGRAM 27

DIAGRAM 28

DIAGRAM 29

DIAGRAM 30

64

edges, and stick them against the thin edges of the model.

The bird, top left, has a cardboard tube protruding from each side of the body for a centre filling. On each end of this tube is stuck a long strip of paper which has been folded at intervals along its length to suggest feathers. Two extra lengths of paper are added to the tail ends. The beak is a piece of shaped paper folded into three sections.

The bird, top right, has two strands of paper running from the chest to the underside of the tail. On these are stuck a small fan shape and a stylized wing. The upper tail has a pointed piece added; the lower shape is cut to a stump. The beak is formed as in diagram 29.

The bird, centre left, has a large paper ring for filling. The wings are two wide triangles of paper, each folded in half and stuck on the side of the body. The beak is made as in diagram 29. The forked tail is an extra length of paper.

The bird, centre right, has eyes constructed as in diagram 30. The body is a panel cut with a curved edge from tail to centre and folded outwards to form a wing. The tail is enlarged with two rounded ends of paper to echo the wing shape. The beak is a piece of shaped paper folded in three sections.

The bird, bottom left, has an eye and beak as in diagram 29. The head is tilted to point the beak upwards. The upper tail is elongated with a splayed shape. The wings are two halves of a wide triangle, stuck point to point on the back.

The bird, bottom right, is tilted upwards from its base. An extra strap of card is stuck at the base of the head and ends in a splayed tail. This tail is stuck with gumstrip to the stump of the original one. The body has four curved pieces of paper, starting below the chest and curving under this extra strap. The eye is a brass fastener wedged in the centre of a coil of paper which is stuck inside the head.

suggestions

A variation for the beak shapes is a sharply pointed cone of paper held in position with tabs of gumstrip.

Those birds which are unsupported between the legs,

could be made more rigid by sticking them to a cardboard base of a suitable geometric shape.

Make a perching bird by standing the body on end and using the wing tips for legs. Elongate them and block them in with panels. Place the head a little to the right on top of the chest, and add beak, wings, tail, etc.

For a flying bird, place the body in a horizontal position. Stick the head well over on the front curve and add all the details. Keep the body with a hollow filling in order to find the balance when suspending the bird with thread. To do this, hold a needle or compass point inside the top curve of the body and balance the bird until the correct flying position is achieved; pierce the card at this point and pull a thread through the body. A small piece of matchstick tied on the end of the thread holds more reliably than a knot. The bird must be completely decorated first.

Reduce all the basic measurements by half and make myriads of small flying and perching birds to decorate a painted branch or frond of evergreen.

Take sheets of cardboard and stick shiny metallic papers on each side. From these construct flying birds in two or three sizes. Thread a number of birds at spaced intervals on to a length of carpet thread and hang them in the well of a staircase. If possible illuminate them from below. The threads should be pulled taut and not allowed to become entangled in a draught. Two stout garden canes nailed in a cross could hold the threads in position at both the top and bottom, and the base must be anchored.

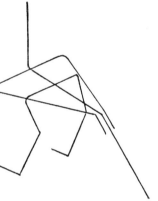

DIAGRAM 31

wire frame birds with metal or cardboard filling

PLATES 15, 19 AND 20

These birds are constructed with a frame made from three lengths of wire each 18 *in* long, which are bound together with fine wire.

The first piece is bent into a long pointed triangle as in diagram 31; this forms the width of the body.

The second piece is bent to include the neck, spine and long tail as in diagram 31.

PLATE 21

PLATE 22

The third piece is bent to form the legs as in diagram 31.

It will be appreciated that lists of exact measurements are unnecessary for this construction. A good proportion is easily effected within the limits of the 18-*in* lengths of wire. To create a bird with other special characteristics would require these measurements to be altered accordingly.

comments on plates 15, 19 and 20
wire and cardboard birds (plate 15)

The flying bird, above, has the leg wire omitted. The front wire forms the triangular body and is folded back at an angle on each side of the spine. The neck is bent forward, and the tip is bent again to project for a beak. Another length of wire, bent to form the back, and the top of the head, is bound with wire to the tail at one end, and to the beak at the other. Two pieces of wire are fastened to the two corners of the body, and are tied together to overlap on the back of the bird as in diagram 32; these are the framework for the wings. All these wires support panels, as in the illustration.

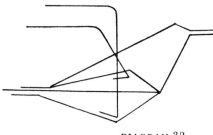

DIAGRAM 32

The standing bird has a head made from a large cork, roughly cut to shape and smoothed with sandpaper. Into it are wedged the two ends of a loop of wire shaped like a neck, as in diagram 33. This special shape is wired to the basic shape and filled in with overlapping tabs of gumstrip. The bird's chest is rounded; the neck is wedged between the chest and leg wire behind it. Leg and foot shapes are bent from single pieces of wire and bound to the leg pieces. They are then wrapped with thin strips of paper brushed with glue. Cardboard body, tail, and wing shapes are stuck to the wires with gumstrip. A cone of paper forms the beak. The eyes are linen washers.

DIAGRAM 33

metal birds (plates 19 and 20)

The standing bird, below, uses the basic body construction with the neck length freely supporting the head. The neck and base of the head are made from a large curved triangle

69

of zinc. The base of the triangle is wired along the leg bar, and the pointed end is held by the neck length. A similar curved triangle of zinc is wired along the chest and is fastened to the tail. A triangle shape is cut from a metal grater, and is wired along the chest, with its pointed end fastened under the head. A similar triangle is wired to the back of the neck and the centre spine. The beak is a zinc garden label, trimmed and bent to shape. The back of the head is a short, narrow triangle of metal. Tail and wing shapes are added. Legs and feet shapes are bent from single pieces of wire and bound to the leg pieces. The eyes are curtain rings, with an inset of metal foil held in position by a brass fastener; these are fastened on to the small head pieces.

The flying bird has a curved chest. The two halves on each side of the spine are bent down, and outwards. The neckline is bent to curve forward, with a second piece of wire curved to form the top of the neck and head. This is wired to the beak and spine respectively. A large triangle of wire is fastened with its base line to the back of the neck and its pointed end to the tail. On to this frame are attached two loops of wire to form the wings. The eye is a glass bead inside a curtain ring. The tail consists of three garden labels cut to shape and wired in position. The body and wings are made from an assortment of meshes of zinc and metal grater.

suggestions

This basic bird shape is still effective when reduced in scale, and can be very imposing when enlarged. It makes a good metalwork subject for schools. Remember that standing birds do not require a base when the tail and feet are used as a tripod support.

Make a bird with a filling of pipe cleaners only, and wire these at narrowly spaced intervals. Brush the whole construction with glue and cover entirely with fine sawdust. Spray with white paint.

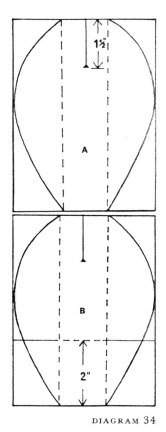

DIAGRAM 34

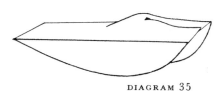

DIAGRAM 35

DIAGRAM 36

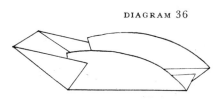

FISH

paper fish

PLATE 21

For this model two measured pieces of paper are required plus extra pieces to use for tail and fins. *A* and *B* are 6 *in* by $4\frac{1}{2}$ *in*.

A is the top half of the fish. Rule lengthways into three equal sections, score the lines for folding, and draw free-hand a curved line in both outside columns. These curves are rounder and fuller at the top edge than at the bottom, and they must also touch the outside edges of the paper. At the top of the centre column rule and cut a line $1\frac{1}{2}$ *in* long, and snip a minute triangle at the end. Cut along both curves and fold the straight lines. Pull the two centre halves to overlap slightly less than $\frac{1}{2}$ *in*, and stick them as in diagram 35.

B is the lower half of the fish, to be cut and stuck in the same way as *A*, after a line has been drawn 2 *in* across the paper at the tail end. This line is folded across the middle section and cut on each side. Check with diagram 34 for layout and 36 for position.

Stick *A* over *B* with a flap of gumstrip to hold the tail end intact. Make the jaws firm with a spot of gum between the cheeks. The tail, cut to any shape, is wedged into the end of the body with three prongs as in diagram 37. Add eyes and fins.

comments on plate 21

The fish here illustrated all retain their essentially stream-lined construction in spite of additional fins and tail pieces. There is much variety in these shapes, but the most telling effects are achieved by the patterns which are painted directly on to heads and bodies. These are simple geometric shapes, used in each case with strongly curved lines which sweep from the open mouths to the backs of the eyes. The curved lines serve to emphasize the distinct portions of heads and bodies, and they also help to relate the eyes to

71

the rest of the design. The eyes are placed to protrude above the sides of the heads, and this is the most effective position for them when viewed from all angles. A refinement of construction is to stick the two halves of the fish together with the lower jaw receding slightly. With all these fish, the three-pronged effect for wedging the tail to the body is used in the upward tilting position. The three prongs may be reversed to hold the tail horizontally. On the centre fish and the two below it, a special platform for holding extra fin shapes is made on the side of the body by slitting and folding outwards the two-pointed end of shape *A* in diagram 34. The smallest of the three fishes shows this shape clearly. The other two have fin shapes attached to them. All the fishes are made with cartridge paper.

DIAGRAM 37

suggestions

This design is used to best effect when the fish is suspended on a thread. An original idea would be to use it as a decorative container for a very special message, written on a long and narrow strip of paper, rolled, and popped into the wide mouth. The fish could then be boxed and posted – ideally, to someone overseas.

The design can be reduced in scale, but should not be enlarged, as the subtlety of the head loses its effect. Utilize and adapt the effects for the other fish and bird shapes in the book.

DIAGRAM 38

cardboard fish

PLATE 13

Three pieces of cardboard are required to make this fish. *A* is 14 *in* by 1 *in*. *B* and *C* are each 10 *in* by 1 *in*.

A forms the body and tail. Make a $\frac{1}{2}$-*in* cut 1 *in* from both ends. These cuts are made on opposite sides and slot into each other.

B forms the inside of the body. Measure $1\frac{1}{2}$ *in* from both ends and cut and slot as in *A*. Place *B* inside *A* and stick with glue where the two loops press together.

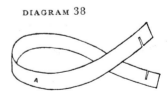

DIAGRAM 39

72

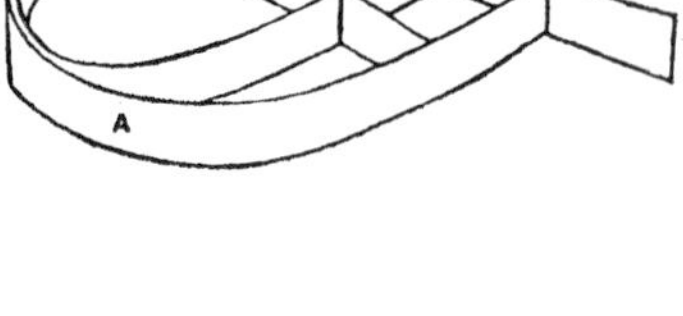

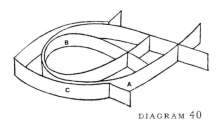

DIAGRAM 40

C forms the head and fins. Measure 1 *in* from both ends, and the half-way line. Score these three lines lightly and fold the two end-pieces outwards to make fins. Lightly curve the two halves inwards from the centre fold and stick in front of *A*. The basic shape is now complete.

comments on plate 13

These three fishes take their variety of design chiefly from the body fillings. The centre fish is left with the body framework clear of any extra pieces. Paper shapes are stuck on the tails, and the fins are long triangles of paper slotted into their stumps. These, together with the eyes, are the only additions. The eye is a large brass paper fastener pierced through a disc of cardboard and wedged into the head. A small fin shape is stuck to one side of the eye.

The top fish has a body filling of card, which includes the snout and encircles the centre loop. To make this, lay the fish flat on a piece of card and draw round the shape required. Cut out and glue the shape, and press it to the narrow edges of the body. The two tail stumps are cut to a point, and they sandwich two leaf shapes which are pressed with a fold along their centres. The fins echo the leaf shape. The eye is made like that of the centre fish but with a more elaborate fin stuck on to it.

The bottom fish has the centre loop and its end filled with panels. A flat leaf shape is stuck on the fin stumps. The tail is elongated with two pieces of folded paper. The eye is a small length of pipe cleaner threaded through the head to hold a cardboard disc and bead, which are glued on each end.

suggestions

There are two methods of supporting this fish. One is to fasten the body on a short rod of dowelling or wire which is then stuck to a wood or cardboard base. The other is to suspend it on a thread – carpet thread. In this case enlarge the proportions of the fish, add lots of details and use it as a wall decoration.

Add long trailing paper fins and tails held in position by wires backed with gumstrip.

Use the surfaces of the inside body shape as platforms on which to stick side projecting fins.

Twist pipe cleaners together to make spikes and fin shapes, and fasten with gumstrip.

wire frame fishes

with cardboard or metal filling

PLATES 23, 24 AND 25

For the construction of these models, the build-up of the head only is given and no measurements are included. Any picture book of fish will show the infinite variety of proportion and scale possible with these creatures, and to pinpoint one set of measurements would be to place a damper on invention. It is suggested, however, that when constructing the head, each of the three triangular shapes should not be be more than 3 *in* long.

In diagram 41, *A* is a narrow triangle of strong cardboard edged on two sides with a piece of wire. The two long ends of wire are left projecting downwards. Gumstrip holds the wire firmly to all the various pieces. *B* is the same, repeated, but with shorter ends of wire, which are upturned and wired to *A*. A third triangle of cardboard, *C*, is wired to have one long end projecting. *C* is then wedged between *A* and *B* with the wire passing under the roof of *A* and held firm with gumstrip; the result is the head of the fish. The three important loose ends of wire are vital for connecting the head to the body. Diagram 42 shows a head constructed to lie horizontal and diagram 43 the wires bent into raised supports for the fish. Compare these last with plates 23, 24 and 25.

comments on plates 23, 24 and 25

A lot of the character in both the cardboard and metal fishes is determined by the tops of their heads, the backs of

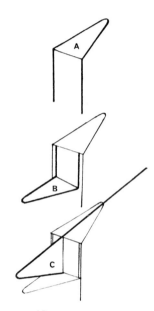

DIAGRAM 41

DIAGRAM 42

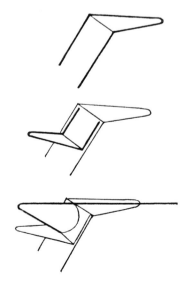

74

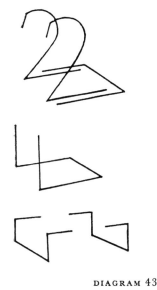

DIAGRAM 43

their snouts, and the size and positioning of their eyes. The interplay of surfaces and voids has to be considered when relating heads to bodies; remember that the gaps require as much attention as the panels. Large areas of cardboard or metal which may look uninteresting in construction can be enlivened with patches of colour or projecting fins.

wire and cardboard fishes

PLATE 23

The centre fish holds its body off the ground with a tripod of two pelvic fins and the anal fin. The tail half of the segmented body is supported by three wires; each side has a wire running the length of the body to the tail, and a third wire stretching from the back of the head to the top of the dorsal fin. The centre section is two hinged triangles which splay outwards to the sides of the lower panel.

The top fish has the front edge of its body wired in the way a flag is attached to a pole. The end of the wire is bent to support the lower panel which is flush with the edge of the jaw. The bottom fish has its snout formed from a diamond shape, divided in the centre by a narrow panel on each side of the head. The triangular body is wired on both its sloping sides, with the projecting ends holding the tail. The wire from the lower sloping edge of this triangle projects to support the horizontal piece, which is connected to the jaw.

metal fishes

PLATES 24 AND 25

Since these are semi-transparent, their construction can be more easily deduced. The eyes of one consist of a length of wire threaded with a bead and encircled with a curtain ring, and with those of the second fish a metal button has been substituted for a bead. The only other materials are zinc, with a large and small mesh, and sixteen gauge wire, which is also used for the cardboard fish.

75

suggestions

These models are suitable for development on quite a large scale, but it should be remembered that the gauge of wire may have to be increased to take the extra weight of the panels. A large metal fish, three feet in length, would require soldered joints and is an ideal subject for the metalwork class in schools.

Fasten together to stand, self-supporting, two or three curving shapes of zinc each with a spine of wire to simulate strands of seaweed. Among them, wire a small metal fish displayed to the best advantage and decorated with jewellery. Lacquer the seaweed black, the fish orange and gold. Place against a blue background.

Make a large fish from cardboard. Fill it with carpet canvas; this tough mesh is an ideal material on which to hang things and, sprayed with gum, it will set rock hard.

Make three or four simple, wire-framed cardboard fishes. Lay them on their sides on a table, grouped in a shoal. Contrive a method of fastening them together at the points where they touch each other, and use as a wall decoration.

Make a very long and narrow wire-framed cardboard fish, paint it with a dynamic geometric pattern, and hang it on a wall.

As a change from flat surfaces, use short lengths of wide cardboard tubing – which are only suitable for the body area. The rings can be used whole or cut in half, and can be stuck vertically or horizontally on each side of a flat body to give a rounded fullness. They make useful surfaces for attaching fins.

PLATE 23

PLATE 24

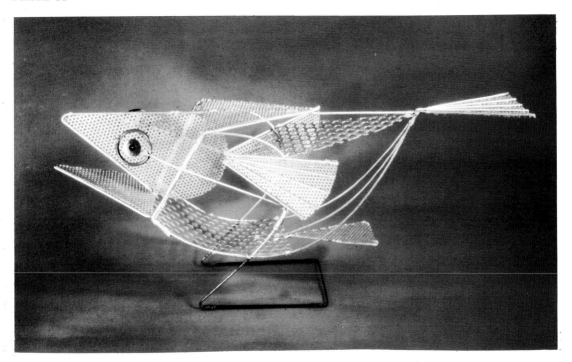

PLATE 25

PLATE 26

PLATE 27

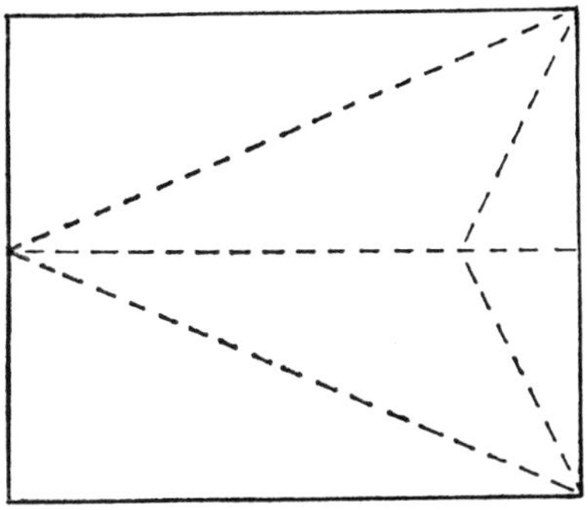

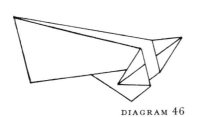

DIAGRAM 44

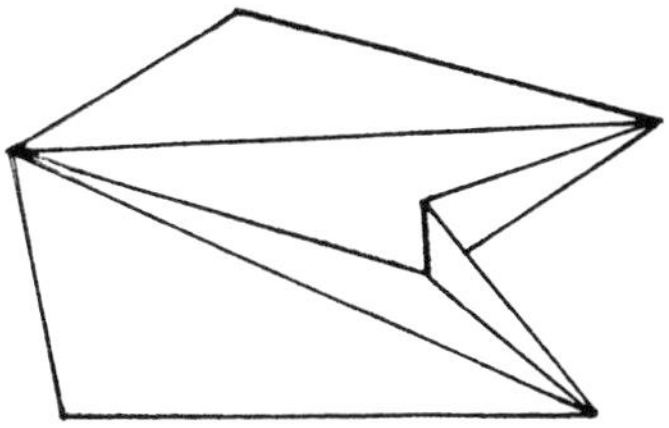

DIAGRAM 45

DIAGRAM 46

INSECT IN PAPER AND WIRE

PLATE 26

For this model, one piece of cartridge paper size 6 *in* by 5 *in* is required; also gumstrip, pieces of wire about 6 *in* in length, and other pieces of paper for details.

Divide the paper lengthways with a centre line, and from the top end draw lines to the bottom left and right corners, as in diagram 44. On the centre line, measure $1\frac{1}{4}$ *in* from the base, and draw two shorter lines to the two corners. This layout forms an arrow head, as in diagram 44. Score all these lines for folding.

Fold the two halves of the paper together and tuck in the small fold as in 45.

The head is made from the two sharply-pointed ends of the paper. Along both the top folds of these points measure $1\frac{1}{2}$ *in* and bend the points outwards as in 46. Two small folds of paper behind these pointed areas are cut, to allow the points to be folded forward and so create the head shape, as in the illustration.

The legs are attached to two small flaps on the underside of the body; first, make two short cuts 1 *in* apart, then separate this piece by slitting it, bend the two flaps outwards, and strengthen the flaps with gumstrip. Make legs by sandwiching lengths of wire between two pieces of gumstrip, and trim them to the required length and thickness.

comments on plate 26

It is well to remember that insect bodies are segmented with very narrow connecting parts between the large shapes. Aim for such an effect with shapes broad enough to be painted with effective markings. The eyes for these insects are made from linen washers stuck on to tabs of gumstrip.

The insect, top left, is made from a piece of paper $7\frac{1}{2}$ *in* long and 5 *in* wide. A vertical piece of paper is slotted between the two halves of the body and decorated.

81

The insect, top right, is $6\frac{1}{2}$ *in* long and 5 *in* wide. It has paper fringes on the legs to suggest hairs, and antennae-like shapes at the back of the head which are constructed in a similar manner. The proboscis is a folded piece of paper wedged and stuck between the two halves of the head.

The lower insect is $8\frac{1}{4}$ *in* long and 6 *in* wide. It has a body with four rows of spines. These are curved pieces of paper, cut into large points with the opposite ends folded into a long narrow tab for sticking on to the body. Each wing is made from three pieces of wire, bent to the required shape and laid in position on a piece of cellophane. The wires are stuck to it with tabs of Sellotape until the whole wing area is covered with them. Many pieces overlay each other. The actual wing shape is then cut out. Make the narrow ends long enough to stick under the body, and bend the wing shape upwards. Decorate the wings.

suggestions

Make winged insects with measurements reduced by half. Stick pieces of jewellery to the body and use, with foliage, for table decoration. Copy the wide variety of body shapes from illustrated insect books. Stick tufts of fur or bristles to the bodies to heighten an effect. Make these models with an eye to creating science fiction shapes, and possibly use them in trick photography to dwarf the human size.

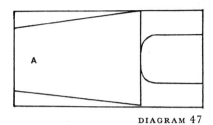

DIAGRAM 47

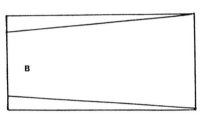

DIAGRAM 48

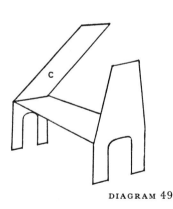

DIAGRAM 49

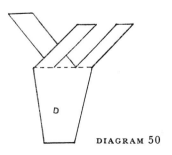

DIAGRAM 50

BULL IN CARDBOARD

PLATE 16

Five pieces of cardboard are required to make this animal: *A* and *B* are 6 *in* by 3 *in*, *C* 2 *in* by 9 *in*, *D* 4 *in* by 2 *in* and *E* 3 *in* by 1 *in*.

Letter these pieces for easy reference.

A forms the chest and front legs. Measure a 2-*in* strip from one of the narrow ends. Inside it, cut a flat arch shape to form the legs. From the top of the legs cut a tapering shape which is 2 *in* wide at the opposite end, as in diagram 47.

Take *B*. Cut it to a tapering shape 3 *in* wide at one end and 2 *in* at the other, as in diagram 48. On the 3-*in* side stick a flap of gumstrip, and stick this end flush with the top of the legs on *A*.

Take *C* and mark off a 3-*in* section from one end. In this space cut out legs $\frac{1}{2}$ *in* wide and $2\frac{1}{2}$ *in* long. Stick the loose end of *B* on this 3-*in* length, which is scored and folded. Stick the loose end of *C* to the top end of *A* with gumstrip, as in diagram 49.

Take *D* and rule this rectangle into two squares. Score and fold this line, and cut the top square into three sections, comprising the back of the neck and two ears. The bottom square is the face, cut to taper at the lower end.

Attach the loose end of the neck to the top of the shoulders with gumstrip. Stick a tab of gumstrip on each end of *E* and stick one end of the front legs and the other behind the face, as in plate 16. Trim and add details.

comments on plate 16

The top bull has its body encased between two side panels, made from cardboard cut to shape. Lay the constructed bull on its side on a piece of cardboard, and draw round the shape required. Cut out these panels and stick them in position with gumstrip; they make a splendid surface for decorating. The bodies of the two bulls below have been left hollow, and the inside areas are decorated.

The extra pieces added to the basic shapes are tails, horns – effectively curved – nostrils and eyes. The tails and horns are cardboard. It is possible to give variety by turning the forward projecting ears into horns, and by sticking the ears on the end of the neck. The nostrils are a small flattened loop of paper or gumstrip stuck on the lower edge of the face. The eyes are linen washers held in position with tabs of gumstrip. All these models are made with medium-strength cardboard.

suggestions

To give a greater degree of permanence to these bulls when they are painted, lightly brush all the surface with liquid glue; but remember that too much brushing with the liquid will loosen and smear the water colour surface. When the gum is completely dry, give the model two coats of clear varnish, allowing for a drying period between each coat. To use this model as a gift holder, use strong cardboard and leave the body hollow. Wrap a gift and pack it into the body area. Then secure it with a coloured cord and decorative label.

It is possible to make the head three-dimensional by sticking narrow triangles of cardboard at right angles along the two sloping sides of the face.

HORSE IN CARDBOARD AND METAL

PLATES 17 AND 18

The main measurements for the framework, neck and chest of a horse of manageable proportions are given in the diagrams 51–53. It would be a laborious business for a beginner to create his or her own measurements. The build-up of the animal is shown in stages; the shaded parts in diagram 53 give a sequence of construction starting with a simple bracket shape for the chest, which is wired to the body frame. Each new piece fastened to this frame is shown shaded.

DIAGRAM 51

DIAGRAM 52

comments on plates 17 and 18

These two horses, one in cardboard and one in metal, have almost identical construction. One difference is the placing of the neck on the body. In both, the front edge of the neck is wired to have a length projecting below it, and this piece is fastened in one case to the right, and in the other to the left side of the chest; the base line of the neck rests across the centre panel, and one end of the mane is tied to one of the body wires. The effect shows clearly on the metal animal. Another difference is in the leg construction. With both horses the width of the legs is made by running a thickness of metal or cardboard from the front of the chest, down to the ground. The thickness behind the legs on the metal horse is obtained by adding a strip of metal wired on both

85

edges; it is bent forward at the top and bottom, and the protruding wires at the lower end are threaded through holes in the leg and bent into hoof shapes. Both fore and hind legs are treated this way, as in the illustration. The cardboard model has four thicknesses of card stuck together and bound to the backs of the legs with gumstrip; cardboard hoofs are stuck in position with glue, and the top end of the neck requires cutting, to take the curved head shape. This animal is easily the most painstaking model in the book, chiefly because four legs have to be negotiated instead of two for a bird or human being.

suggestions

The most interesting way to create an effect different from that of the horses in the illustration is to alter the shape of the neck. Consider an arched neck with the head pointing downwards as in a grazing position.

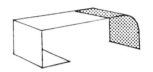

Try tilting the head backwards to point the nose upwards.

The ears may be pointed back from the head.

The tail may be improvised.

The cardboard horse may be decorated like a circus horse.

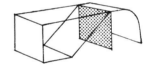

Both animals could be given riders in cardboard or metal, but these should be constructed as simply as possible.

DIAGRAM 53

CARDBOARD WALL FIGURES

PLATE 22

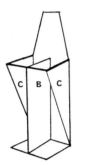

DIAGRAM 54

The basic construction for this figure requires four pieces of cardboard: A is 10 *in* by $2\frac{1}{2}$ in, B and C are $5\frac{1}{2}$ *in* by 2 *in*, and D is $4\frac{1}{2}$ *in* by 4 *in*. Additional pieces of cardboard are required, and also some thin card.

A forms the back and base of the figure. From one end measure a strip 2 *in* wide. Score and fold this line to make a base. $5\frac{1}{2}$ *in* from this base cut two inclined edges to form an end piece $1\frac{1}{2}$ *in* wide.

B and C are robe shapes. Using gumstrip, stick shape B in the centre of A. Cut panel C in half diagonally, and stick these two pieces with gumstrip on the outside edges of A. All three pieces are secured along their top edges with a strip of wire as in diagram 55. The centre panel has its top corner wired to this support.

D forms the arms and shoulders. From one end measure a panel 2 *in* wide. Score and fold the line. Cut the other half of the cardboard with tapering sides to make an end piece 2 *in* wide. Cut cardboard sleeve shapes and stick them in position as in diagram 56. This shape is stuck flush with the top edge of A. A sloping front panel supports shape D on the underside, as in plate 22. A small panel is hinged from the top of the shoulders and is supported underneath with a small vertical panel, as in the illustration. The head is cut from an elongated box shape of thin card as in diagram 57.

DIAGRAM 55

DIAGRAM 56

comments on plate 22

The two figures here are designed with a flat back which allows them to hang flush against a wall. A small hole is made directly behind the front panel of the head or stomach so that the figure can be hung on a short nail or pot hook. It is best viewed a little below eye-level, for then the greatest number of surfaces are displayed to the best advantage. The figures have an essentially period flavour, determined by their robes. The fisherman is given an angular chest and

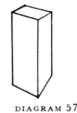

DIAGRAM 57

hat to create a masculine effect. The woman with a bird is given panels with curved edges to create a feminine appearance. Two strips of paper fall from each side of the waist and curve to the back of this figure; the conical hat has curling shapes of thin card, and a bead and cardboard disc are threaded with a pipe cleaner and wedged into the cone. The hands for both figures are thin pieces of card cut and folded at the basic hand joints. The thumbs are bent over to stick at right angles. The noses are folded card glued into position. Eyes and mouths are painted.

METAL FREE-STANDING FIGURE

PLATE 27

The metal figure, constructed from pieces of perforated zinc and wire, is free standing. The body and robe have the same basic construction as the cardboard wall figures. The base is elongated at the back. The head is a wide shield shape curved and wired to the neck. The back of the crown is a spoon shape made of zinc. The front area is large-mesh zinc, cut into three small pyramids. A bent triangle of zinc forms the nose, and an added piece of wire runs round the inside of the face. The hands have bent wire fingers, and the palms a filling of zinc.

suggestions

Give these figures shapes or objects to hold which will help to emphasize their character.

When making a figure, tilt the head forward slightly to make the eyes look down at the hands. This will soften any stiffness of posture and display a headdress to full effect.

Oriental, historical and religious figures are the best subjects for this type of model.

INVENTORY 74

SPRING 78

INVENTORY 1983

CITIZEN REX

CITIZEN

Story and Art by

MARIO & GILBERT HERNANDEZ

DARK HORSE BOOKS™

REX

WHY?

Editor
DIANA SCHUTZ

Assistant Editor
BRENDAN WRIGHT

Book Design
JUSTIN COUCH

Digital Production
RYAN HILL

Publisher
MIKE RICHARDSON

This book collects issues one through six of Citizen Rex, originally published July through
December 2009 by Dark Horse Comics.

Library of Congress Cataloging-in-Publication Data on file.

Published by Dark Horse Books
A division of Dark Horse Comics, Inc.
10956 SE Main Street
Milwaukie, Oregon 97222

DarkHorse.com

First edition: June 2011
ISBN 978-1-59582-556-8

1 3 5 7 9 10 8 6 4 2

Printed at Midas Printing International, Ltd., Huizhou, China

frontispiece art by **JAIME HERNANDEZ**

During the early stages of this project, I mulled over an encounter with a science fiction fan at a convention:

The fan introduced me to a friend as "one of the *Love and Rockets* brothers." The other friend snorted, "*Love and Rockets* is nothing but a soap opera." I gave him my friendliest shrug and said, "But it's a well-drawn soap opera!"

What I meant to say was, "So is most science fiction, really."

Gilbert and I have worked on many projects together, with a lot of the same sort of trappings: *Mister X* (with brother Jaime); *Tales of Somnopolis*; various shorter works for *Love and Rockets*; and our larger opus, "Me for the Unknown," in the second volume of the *L&R* series. This wasn't science fiction. (Although people wrote about it like it was.) It was basically a family drama, people trapped in a whirlwind of large human events. *Citizen Rex* has some of the same elements. Good intentions, bad decisions, peripheral characters, and events that make the story jump.

So we have the saga of CTZ-RX-1. An exercise in human/robot allegory. The fine threads of fate clinging and breaking away, as the players pinball through the maze of situations and obstacles I've thrown at them. In other words, business as usual in Hernandezland.

We hope you get a kick out of it as much as we did, bringing it to you.

—Mario Hernandez

OUR FAIR
CITY.

AND AS IN MOST
CITIES, SOMETIMES THE
MORE INTERESTING
STORIES HAPPEN BEHIND
CLOSED DOORS.

7

IT'S 3 A.M. IN THE SOUTH CIVIC PLAZA, AND TONIGHT I'VE BEEN SPIT ON, HIT ON THE BACK WITH A BOTTLE, AND WORST OF ALL:

DOGPILED ON!

3 A.M., THE DEEPEST PART OF THE NIGHT. MOST BARS AND BISTROS HAVE SHED THEIR PATRONS.

CRAP!

WHERE ARE MY SHOES?

TAGG LILLARD BISTRO

Le FOU

A FEW STRAGGLERS WITH THEIR HAUNTED EYES SLOWLY PINBALL THEIR WAY DOWN SILENT STREETS.

VAMPIRE SCENE-MAKERS START TO WANDER HOME BEFORE THE BREAK OF DAWN.

MUGGED OR BASHED, HARDLY SEEMS RELEVANT. I HURT LIKE HELL.

TSK. DID THEY HAVE TO TRASH HER, TOO? NEITHER OF US PUT UP MUCH OF A FIGHT!

I NEED TO HELP HAZEL, MY ROBOT ASSISTANT. I'VE HAD HER SINCE I WAS ELEVEN YEARS OLD.

WHAT THE HELL HAPPENED TO MY SHOES?

I AM SERGIO BAUNTIN.

YES, OF THE FILTHY BOURGEOIS BAUNTINS.

I WRITE THE POPULAR WEB COLUMN "THE 3 O'CLOCK" UNDER THE NOM-DE-GUERRE "BLOGGO."

I SPECIALIZE IN THE DEBUNKING OF RUMORS AND URBAN LEGENDS IN OUR FAIR CITY, AS WELL AS IN TAKING SOME WELL-AIMED POT-SHOTS AT OUR ELITE SOCIETY SWELLS ON OCCASION.

CITIZEN REX
I WAS ON STAKEOUT, INVESTIGATING THE MYSTERIOUS APPEARANCE OF THIS LARGE CHUNK OF UNKNOWN MATTER, PLUNKED HERE BY WHO-KNOWS-WHO OR WHY.
BUT THEN, OUR CITY FATHERS OFTEN INSTALL CIVIC ART THIS WAY.
WHY?

OH, HELL! HERE COMES A SQUAD OF TRUTH TAKERS!

NOT EXACTLY THE POLICE (THE POLICE ARE NOT AS BAD), THEY ARE COMMISSIONED BY THE CITY TO BE SORT OF AUTONOMOUS INVESTIGATOR - HISTORIANS.

I COULD BE HELD FOR DAYS OR WEEKS BY THESE PEOPLE-- OR DISAPPEAR FOR EVEN LONGER (THAT'S IF THEY'RE NOT SATISFIED WITH THE "TRUTH" YOU GIVE THEM, EVEN IF IT'S THE REAL TRUTH).

THE MECH TECHS HERE AT THE CONSCIOUSNESS CLINIC DO EXPERT WORK. THEY KEEP HAZEL FOR A FEW HOURS, AND THEY ASSURE ME THAT HER MEMORY FILES ARE ALL INTACT.

TAKE HER DOWN TO THE RECHARGE LOUNGE AND SHE'LL BE GOOD AS NEW.

THANKS.

I HAVE A COLUMN DUE IN A FEW HOURS.

THE RECHARGE LOUNGE IS THE BEST PLACE TO GET REALLY JUICY GOSSIP (PLUS, YOU CAN STILL SMOKE IN THERE).

LUCKILY, I SPY THE TWO TRUTH TAKERS SKULKING AROUND THE HALL. I SEND HAZEL TO THE ELEVATOR ALONE.

HAZEL GOES TO STEP INTO THE RECHARGE LOUNGE, AND A T.T. AMBUSHES HER BY JABBING A PROBE IN HER MEMORY PORT! NOW I'LL HAVE TO NOT BE HOME FOR A WHILE.

IT'LL TAKE THE TRUTH TAKERS A FEW HOURS TO PROCESS AND COLLATE WHAT HAZEL'S SEEN.

JUST MY LUCK! IN MY RUSH TO CATCH UP TO HAZEL, I KNOCK DOWN A DOMESTIC ROBOT! LUCKILY, THE OWNER DOESN'T PRESS CHARGES, AND SECURITY DOESN'T GET INVOLVED. I'M IN ENOUGH TROUBLE WITH MY FATHER (WHEN HE GETS THE BILL FOR HAZEL).

IT'S NOT THE FIRST TIME I'VE GOTTEN MIXED UP WITH TRUTH TAKERS. IF THEY EVER CATCH UP WITH ME, I'M T.T. TOAST.

WHICH MADE IT ALL THE MORE URGENT TO GET BACK TO THE PAD TO DO SOME CLEANING UP AND GENERATE A COLUMN BEFORE DEADLINE.

THE BLOOFER APARTMENTS.

IN MY STILL WOOZY STATE, I ENTERED MY APARTMENT AND NOTICED LARGE HULKING SHADOWS LOOMING ALONG THE WALLS.

WE NEED TO GET RIGHT TO WORK, HAZEL, BEFORE THE T.T.'S COME AND--

WHAT'S THAT SMELL...?

12

13

I'D HEARD OF HIM ALL RIGHT, AND IF I WANTED TO LIVE THROUGH THIS, I'D BETTER EAT THE SOUP.

I'M NOT SURE HOW LONG HE TALKED ABOUT PROSTHETICS AND THE BLACK MARKET (?), OR HOW MUCH SOUP I ATE, BUT DESPITE MY WOOZINESS FROM THE NIGHT'S EVENTS, I MANAGED TO HOLD FAST.

I KNEW HAZEL WAS FILMING AND RECORDING BANGAREE'S EVERY WORD.

THEN THEY WERE GONE.

OK, SO BETWEEN LOAN SHARKING, SMUGGLING, FORGING, AND KIDNAPPING, MR. BANGAREE IS GETTING INTO THE PROSTHETIC LIMB RACKET.

THAT'S THE MOST DANGEROUS END OF THE BLACK MARKET THESE DAYS.

BUT WHAT MAKES HIM THINK I KNOW ANYTHING THAT COULD HELP HIM?

MY MEMORY ARCHIVE TELLS ME THAT YOU WROTE SEVERAL COLUMNS ABOUT THAT VERY SUBJECT APPROXIMATELY 765 COLUMNS AGO.

DO A HIGHLIGHTED SURVEY FOR ME. I AM NOT UP FOR HEAVY RESEARCH. ALL OF THAT OLD DATA IS PROBABLY OBSOLETE!

MOREOVER, MR.B., WHOM DO YOU SUPPOSE THIS BELONGS TO?

17

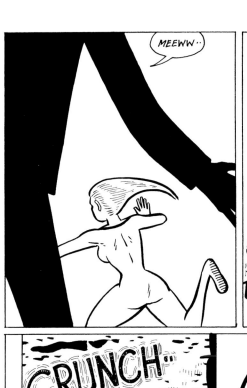

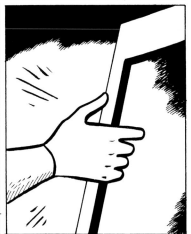

24

SHOOP!

WELL!

HOW LONG HAS THIS SECRET DOORWAY BEEN HERE?

FZZZT BZZT

WHOEVER YOU ARE--

BZZZT
FZZZZT

PROLOGUE: The 3 O'CLOCK by BLOGGO

TIMELINE!

"*GRA* INDUSTRIES, 25 YEARS AGO.

"PRESIDENT MULDOON SIGNS THE SYNTHETIC RIGHTS AMENDMENT, GIVING GRA IND. AN EXCLUSIVE CONTRACT TO RESEARCH AND DEVELOP ADVANCED ROBOTICS.

"SCIENTISTS DEVELOP THE FIRST CONSCIOUSNESS CHIP, AND ROBOT COMPANIONS BECOME THE RAGE.

STICKERS

"ROBOT CTZ-RX-1 IS THE FIRST MODEL TO SHOW SIGNS OF 'NATURAL' BEHAVIOR. 'CITIZEN REX' BEGINS THE FUTURE!

"*HIS* PUBLIC DEBUT IS A GALA EVENT. POLITICOS AND CELEBS ARE ENTHRALLED.

"STATE-OF-THE-ART PLAS-DERMIS MAKES HIM THE MOST HUMAN-LIKE SYNTHETIC TO DATE.

"'REX,' AS HE IS KNOWN, MIXES IN WITH THE ELITE, AS TOAST OF THE TOWN.

"OLD-FASHIONED SCANDAL BRINGS REX DOWN.

"A KINKY AFFAIR WITH FETED SOCIALITE RENATA SKINK TEARS THE CITY APART.

"THE SORDID TRIAL PUTS THE LID ON SYNTHETIC LIFE, PARTIAL AND OTHERWISE.

"REX IS DEACTIVATED IN SECRET AND HIS WHEREABOUTS UNKNOWN UNTIL NOW.

"ARE WE READY FOR A REX REVIVAL?"

CITIZEN REX

WATER! ELECTRICITY! MEAT!

by MARIO and BETO - 2008

REX

THE TOWN WAS GOING CRAZY--JUST LIKE THE OLD DAYS! INNOVATION IN ROBOTICS WAS BACK IN VOGUE. MY MENTION OF THE UPTOWN SIGHTING OF CTZ-RX-1 RE-UNLEASHED THE OLD HYSTERIA!

HAZEL AND I WERE OUT FOLLOWING UP ON SOME OF THE MORE INTERESTING WITNESSES.

CORONARY DE GROOT-- OCCUPATION: BUM.

HE STOLE MY SHOES WHILE I WAS ASLEEP IN AN ALLEY.

I SAW HIM JUST TEN MINUTES AGO ON THE TRANSWAY!

TINY CONTRERAS-- OCCUPATION: MOPPET.

MY GRANDMA SAW HIM IN OUR LAUNDRY BASEMENT, TRYING ON HER UNDA DRAWS.

DORCAS JANE SELWIN-- OCCUPATION: DOWAGER.

MY MAID AND NEW CHAUFFEUR CAUGHT HIM FILCHING GROCERIES IN THE GARAGE.

THEY SAY HE'S VERY GOOD-LOOKING.

SIGMUND SKINK-- OCCUPATION: LAB TECH.

HE HAS A SECRET LABORATORY BEHIND THE WALL, BUT I CAN'T FIND THE DOORWAY TO IT.

HE GOT AWAY AS I WAS CALLING SECURITY.

32

33

35

As Hazel and I make our exit without too much incident, "Citizen Rex" is still at large!

But what can the mysterious man/machine be up to?

What compels life without a soul?

WHY?

WHY?

I found Rex, Mambo!

He's--

Wait! Boss, he was here--

TIN MAN.

WE NEED TO TALK.

THERE IS ANOTHER 3 O'CLOCK THAT CAN BE JUST AS SILENT AND FORBIDDING AS THE NIGHT.

THIS IS THE QUIET 3:00 IN THE AFTERNOON THAT IS NAP TIME, SIESTA TIME, THE TIME WHEN YOU'RE FALLING ASLEEP AT YOUR DESK, OR SIMPLY WATCHING THE CLOCK FOR SCHOOL TO LET OUT.

SOMETIMES WHILE LYING OR SITTING IN A DARKENED ROOM, WATCHING THE DUST MOTES SLOWLY SWIRLING IN A SHAFT OF AFTERNOON LIGHT, THERE COMES A CERTAIN CLARITY OF THOUGHT.

SOME GOOD IDEAS MAY EVEN CREEP IN.

NOT ALL IS SERENE AT THIS TIME, OF COURSE; THE WORLD IS GOING FULL TILT IN SOME QUARTERS.

IN THIS WEEK'S CLIMATE OF MISTRUST AND PARANOIA OVER THE SIGHTING OF ROBOT MODEL CTZ-RX-1, FACTIONS ARE DRAWING LINES IN THE SAND OVER THE RIGHTS OF WEMs ("WATER! ELECTRICITY! MEAT!" ALL THE GOOD STUFF THAT MAKES HUMANS WHAT THEY ARE!) TO GET THE LATEST IN DESIGNER PROSTHETIC LIMBS. (HATE THOSE MANKY TOES AND BUNIONS THAT HAVE PLAGUED YOU ALL YOUR LIFE? WELL, LOP 'EM OFF AND GET WHOLE NEW FEET!)

BANGAREE IS TAKING A LITTLE VACATION. HE LEFT ME IN CHARGE.

I'VE GOT AN ASSIGNMENT FOR YOU, RENATA. YOU CAN MEET WITH REX AGAIN, NO? FOR ME, FOR OLD TIMES' SAKE?

I'M NOT DOING ANYTHING FOR YOU, MAMBO! GIVE ME MY MONEY, SO I CAN--

YOU NEED A SESSION WITH THE EYE, RENATA.

M-MAMBO, NOT THE EYE, PLEASE!

I FREAK OUT FOR DAYS WHEN THE EYEEEEEEEEEEEAAA AAAAAAA AEEEEE

GRA INDUSTRIES
"YOUR GOOD RIGHT ARM"

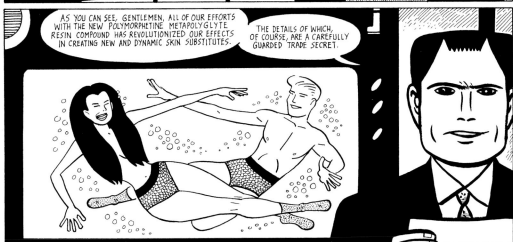

AS YOU CAN SEE, GENTLEMEN, ALL OF OUR EFFORTS WITH THE NEW POLYMORPHETINE METAPOLYGLYTE RESIN COMPOUND HAS REVOLUTIONIZED OUR EFFECTS IN CREATING NEW AND DYNAMIC SKIN SUBSTITUTES.

THE DETAILS OF WHICH, OF COURSE, ARE A CAREFULLY GUARDED TRADE SECRET.

BZZZ⚡ZZZT..

THERE, NATWICK. BETTER THAN NEW!

CAN WE TALK IN PRIVATE?

MY BOYS WON'T SELL OUT OUR SECRETS, MR. CHUFTAN-- THEY CAN'T SPEAK OR WRITE.

OK, BOYS, BACK TO WORK.

I KEEP FORGETTING THAT MOST OF YOUR STAFF ARE SYNTHETICS.

LOOK, WE HAVE A SERIOUS SITUATION WITH CTZ-RX-1 BEING ON THE LOOSE! YOU GAVE ME YOUR GUARANTEE THAT REVIVING HIM WOULD BE A GOOD IDEA, AND NOW HE'S OUT MAKING HEADLINES AND SCARING THE CRAP OUT OF PEOPLE.

"ISN'T HE AMAZING? HE STARED AT ME WITH THOSE BEAUTIFUL EYES AS I IMPLANTED THE NEW BRAIN CHIPS. HE ACTUALLY SMILED AND WALKED ABOUT THE ROOM. NO, GLIDED!"

45

46

LOOK AT THIS PLACE!

ARE THESE SPARE PARTS?

THIS APPEARS TO BE THE MECHANISM TO ACHIEVE THE ILLUSION OF HUMAN SKIN, AND THIS QUAINT CHARACA-TRACER TRANSFERS INFORMATION TO THE CORTEX OF THIS CHILD'S MASK FABRICATOR.

THIS PSEUDO-SKIN IS A FASCINATING ORGANO-SYNTHETIC HYBRID MATERIAL UNKNOWN TO MY MEMORY BANKS.

SOUNDS INTRIGUING.

"POLYMORPHETINE METAPOLYGLYTE."

I WATCHED HIM GET IN THAT SUIT AND MARINATE HIMSELF INTO THE *SPITTIN'* IMAGE OF A YOUNG HENRY SKINK.

INTO MY FATHER?

BUT WHY?

SHOOMP!

BECAUSE THAT FREAKIN' REX DOESN'T KNOW HOW TO TAKE NO FOR AN ANSWER.

49

BUT-- BUT... THE TRUTH TAKERS! HOW DID YOU MANAGE TO KEEP FROM CAPTURE, MS. SKINK?

THAT CREW WASN'T THE T.T.'s. THOSE WERE MAMBO'S BOYS LOOKING FOR REX.

I THINK THAT'S THE LAST WE'LL SEE OF REX. MAMBO'S GOT BIG PLANS FOR HIM.

ANYONE FOR A DRINK?

THE BOYS?!

HEY, THEY FORGOT ME! MAKE WAY!

?

I DIDN'T KNOW YOUR UNCLE'S A GANGSTER.

FOR A SECOND THERE, I THOUGHT YOUR DAD WAS A ROBOT.

AH, BUT REX IS SO MUCH MORE.

ONCE YOU GET TO KNOW HIM, YOU CAN'T HELP BUT GET SUCKED INTO HIS WORLD.

MAMBO HAD TO SCRAMBLE MY BRAINS TO GET ME INVOLVED AGAIN, THE BASTARD.

IT TOOK ALL MY WILL-POWER TO GET YOU TWO OVER HERE.

HOW 'BOUT THAT DRINK?

AHA!

HOMING DEVICE ONLY IN THE WRIST!

I WON'T MAKE THAT MISTAKE AGAIN!

WHOA, THIS EYE IS REALLY COOL!

GRA

YOU TWO GO TO THE BIG MYSTERY "BLOCK" AND WAIT FOR REX THERE!

IF HE'S STILL MOSTLY IN ONE PIECE, THAT'S WHERE HE'LL PROBABLY RETURN.

BUT JUST IN CASE, THIS MONITOR ACCESSES WHAT REX IS SEEING! WE CAN SHUT DOWN HIS BLINKING PROTOCOL!

OK, THIS MAY HELP US FIGURE OUT HOW HE ENDED UP WITH THE SUPPLY OF POLY-META AND THE SCIENCE TO USE IT!

I'M REALLY LOVING THIS EYE!

WE CAN CHECK IT OUT BACK AT THE LAB.

VÁMONOS, MUCHACHOS!

YEAH, THE TRUTH TAKERS HAD A TRACKER BEAM ON US AND THEN QUIT CHASING US, TIN MAN.

JUST DISAPPEARED INTO THE SMOG!

YOU NEVER CAN TELL WHAT'S UP WITH THAT OUTFIT.

NEUTROPOLIS HOSPITAL

THEY'RE JUST ABOUT TO OPERATE. THEY'LL GIVE MAMBO A TEMPORARY EYE UNTIL WE FIND HIS.

LET'S GIVE 'EM THIS EYE. IT'S ONE OF REX'S. I LIFTED IT FROM HIS LAB.

LET'S SEE HOW BOSS MAMBO PUTS IT TO USE.

BRACCO-- HERMANO.

TICO.

THIS SQUARES ME WITH MAMA, RIGHT?

EXCELLENT WORK, MY BROTHER.

YOU'VE EARNED YOUR FORGIVENESS.

GO AND GREET OUR SISTERS.

54

TEE HEE!

SWAK!

THAT WAS FROM MAMA!

OTHERWISE, KEEP UP THE GOOD WORK!

WE NEED YOU TO STICK CLOSE TO MAMBO A LITTLE LONGER!

OH, MY-- A ROBOT PERSON!

A REAL PRETTY ONE!

HEY, THIS IS A DISGUISE!

THANKS FOR COMING.

WE FOUND HIM UNDER THE STRANSKY BRIDGE, FLOPPING AROUND LIKE A BREAKDANCING BARRACUDA.

PEOPLE THROW OUT THE DARNEDEST THINGS.

LET'S SEE IF HE SPARKS UP.

THIS SKIN DOESN'T FEEL LIKE THE USUAL SYN-DERM CRAP!

WOW, HE SUCKS UP POWER FASTER THAN ANY ROBOT I'VE EVER SEEN!

HE'S GOT A WEIRD CLUSTER OF CONSCIOUSNESS CHIPS-- PROBABLY TO KEEP HIM UNDER CONTROL.

I AM CTZ-RX-1!

IT IS IMPERATIVE THAT I BE PUT IN CONTACT WITH MAYOR PARBOYLE MAGNUSSEN, OR MY EXCELLENT FRIEND RENATA SKINK.

MY ARM IS MISSING AND I MUST BE PUT RIGHT.

THE 3 O'CLOCK BY BLOGGO:

"THE LIFE AND MYSTERY OF 'CITIZEN REX,' AS I LIKE TO CALL HIM, IS INTERTWINED WITH THAT OF OUR FORMER MAYOR AND ACTING CEO-CFO OF GRA INDUSTRIES, P. F. MAGNUSSEN, AND VARIOUS SOCIETY PLAYERS AND POSEURS.

"RECENT ENCOUNTERS WITH SOME OF THE PLAYERS HAVE BROUGHT US THUS FAR!"

"REX ROAMS FREELY THROUGH OUR FAIR CITY IN SEARCH OF HIS PAST ACQUAINTANCES AND INSIGNIFICANT OTHERS, DODGING MOBSTERS (IN FOR THE COOL SCIENCE TO BE EXPLOITED FOR CASH), GRA R+D SCIENTISTS (IN FOR THE COOL SCIENCE TO BE EXPLOITED FOR CASH), AND, OF COURSE, THE TRUTH TAKERS, WHO ARE ONLY EVER INTERESTED IN HIS HISS-HISS HISTORY."

"TRUTH TAKERS RECENTLY RAIDED--I'M SORRY, INVESTIGATED--A SECRET LAB LOCATED IN, OF ALL PLACES, THE DOMICILE OF A CERTAIN EX-TABLOID PHENOMENON, SPARKING A FULL-FLEDGED INVESTIGATION (I WONDER WHAT A PARTIALLY FLEDGED ONE WOULD COME UP WITH) BY OUR FAIR CITY FATHERS IN CONJUNCTION WITH (MIRACLE OF MIRACLES) THE CITY'S FINEST-- OUR LACONIC VERSION OF POLICE INVESTIGATORS.

"THEIR TARGET? THE HOW AND WHY OF REX'S RETURN. THE GROWING RANKS OF THE WEM CROWD ALSO WANT A PIECE OF REX TO START A ROBOTS' RIGHTS CAMPAIGN. YEAH, WHO'S GOING TO BE LAME ENOUGH TO JOIN SOMETHING LIKE THAT?"

WATER! ELECTRICITY!! MEAT

YEAH, WHO'S GOING TO BE LAME ENOUGH TO JOIN SOMETHING LIKE THAT?

MR. B., WHICH DO YOU DEEM CORRECT FOR OUR FIRST RALLY?

ROBOTS' RIGHTS

HUMAN IS HUMAN

60

YEAH, A BUNCH OF TOOLS...

AAAND WORKMAN'S STUFF. NOBODY'S WORKIN' T'DAY.

MY ODOR SENSORS ARE DETECTING FAINT TRACES OF...

I WILL GO UP THE LAST LEVEL ALONE.

MAKE SURE ALL SUITS ARE SECURE.

WE LOST REX'S VISUALS!

BOOST THE POWER IN THE BACKUP!

I'M GOING TO ZAP HIM WITH A MAX-JOLT THAT SHOULD BRING HIM BACK ONLINE!

YOU WILL TRANSFER A SUBSTANTIAL BLOCK OF YOUR SUBSIDIARY RESEARCH WING'S STOCK TO A GHOST ACCOUNT.

THESE ARE THE CODES AND NUMBERS YOU WILL NEED.

HAS EVERYONE DONNED A HAZMAT SUIT?

I DETECT VERY TOXIC VAPORS IN THE UPPER CHAMBER. THESE SHOULD HAVE MINIMAL EFFECT ON ME.

WHEN I OPEN THE HATCH, STAY BACK AS FAR AS YOU CAN.

HEY, SO HOW DOES THIS THINGY ATTACH TO THIS THINGY?

I'M NOT HEARING ANY TRANSMISSIONS!

POWER'S UP!

OK, MR. REX, YOU WILL BE MINE ONCE AGAIN!

ALL MINE!

CLICK!

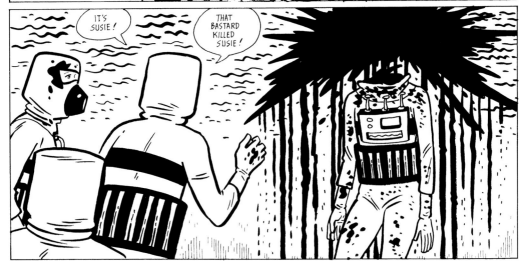

Citizen REX

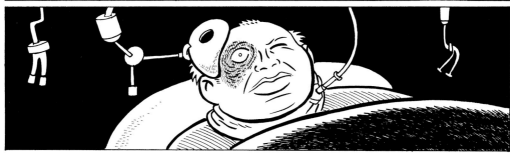

The Truth may Disturb you

TRUTH TAKERS HAVE BEEN SERVING THE COMMUNITY FOR 75 YEARS, FOUNDED BY THE BERRIGAN MONKS AND GIVEN A CITY ORDER TO RECORD AND ARCHIVE EVENTS, AS DID THE ANCIENT ORDERS THROUGHOUT HISTORY.

THE SCARIEST PART OF "ATTENDING" A T.T. INFO-GATHERING, AS THEY CALL IT, IS DEALING WITH THE GOOD AND SINCERE BERRIGAN BROTHERS AS THEY WEND THEIR WAY AROUND YOUR ANSWERS WITH MORE QUESTIONS, SPECULATION, "INSINUENDO," AND THE RANDOM SCARING THE CRAP OUT OF YOU.

HAVING SPENT A FEW UNENLIGHTENING HOURS WITH THE FIRST LINE OF QUESTIONING, I WAS AFRAID IT MIGHT COME TO THIS: THE T.T.s ARE RARELY SATISFIED WITH "I CAN'T REMEMBER," OR "I DIDN'T GET THE MEMO."

I'D HEARD RUMORS ABOUT "CLOUDROOM," BUT NO ONE WHO'S EVER COME OUT OF HERE HAS A VERY CLEAR MEMORY OF IT.

THE NIGHT YOU WERE MUGGED AT THE "BLOCK," WHERE HAD YOU BEEN PREVIOUSLY?

DAMNED IF I COULD REMEMBER WHERE I HAD BEEN, MUCH LESS WHAT HAPPENED BETWEEN LEAVING THE PARTY AND WAKING UP TO A BOTTLE IN THE BACK OF MY HEAD AND GETTING DOGPILED ON.

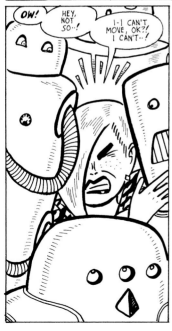

THE YOUNG WOMAN TRAPPED BETWEEN THE CROWD OF ROBOTS AND THE DOORS IS BECOMING MORE AGITATED, AS TRUTH TAKER SECURITY REFUSES TO LET HER INTO THE BUILDING!

WHAT A DEVELOPIN' REVOLT!

OOF!

WEM

ROBOTS' RIGHTS

WHAT THE HELL DO YOU WANT?

WHO--?

REX?!

OH, MY GOD!

GET ME OUT OF HERE!

THIS GUY IS DANGEROUSLY NUTS!!

CITIZENS!

YES, MY ROBOT BROTHERS! YOU ARE EVERY BIT A FELLOW CITIZEN OF THIS MAGNIFICENT METROPOLIS!

MEANWHILE...

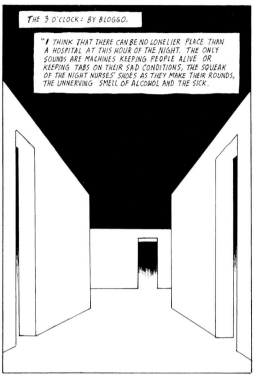

THE 3 O'CLOCK: BY BLOGGO.

"*I* THINK THAT THERE CAN BE NO LONELIER PLACE THAN A HOSPITAL AT THIS HOUR OF THE NIGHT. THE ONLY SOUNDS ARE MACHINES KEEPING PEOPLE ALIVE OR KEEPING TABS ON THEIR SAD CONDITIONS, THE SQUEAK OF THE NIGHT NURSES' SHOES AS THEY MAKE THEIR ROUNDS, THE UNNERVING SMELL OF ALCOHOL AND THE SICK.

"*O*NE CAN ONLY WONDER AT THIS PURGATORY OF MISERY AND HEALING, AND MARVEL AT THE MIRACLES THAT OCCUR CONSTANTLY, CONSISTENTLY.

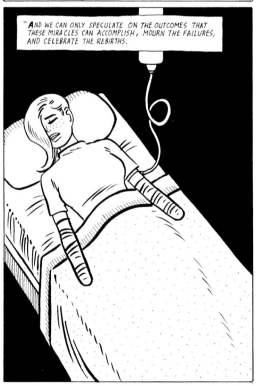

"*A*ND WE CAN ONLY SPECULATE ON THE OUTCOMES THAT THESE MIRACLES CAN ACCOMPLISH, MOURN THE FAILURES, AND CELEBRATE THE REBIRTHS.

"*T*HIS ALSO HOLDS TRUE, MOST EMPHATICALLY, FOR THE INORGANIC, YET STALWART, IN OUR LIVES AS WELL."

87

THE THREE O'CLOCK: BY BLOGGO--
"DOWNTOWN AND AROUND: STILL ROCKING
AND REELING FROM THE BIG SHOCKS
BROUGHT ON BY T.T. SECURITY AND
THE REAL REX APPEARANCE, SWIRLING
UP A TEMPEST OF LAWSUITS AND MORE
PROTESTS. NICE WORK IF YOU CAN GET IT.

"MY OWN SESSIONS? CUT
SHORT BY A MYSTERIOUS
BLACKOUT!"

"NICE PIC-SHOTS OF THE MAYOR AND CHIEF OF PEACE
CONTROL HOT-TUBBING WHILE ROME BURNS. NO REAL
SIGN OF REPERCUSSIONS, SINCE ALL THE BLAME'S BEEN
PILED ONTO 'OUR FAIR SCAPEGOAT':

"CITIZEN
REX.

"SOME ARE TRUCKING AWAY THE REMAINING FEW ERRANT
ROBOTS THAT WERE FUSED TO THE GROUND. OTHERS ARE
SUING T.T. HQ FOR DAMAGES, CAUSING A TEMPORARY LULL
IN T.T. ACTIVITY. QUESTIONS ABOUND:

"WHAT HAS REX ACTUALLY DONE, BESIDES
SCARE THE CRAP OUT OF A FEW PEOPLE
AND BADMOUTH THE POWERS THAT BE?

"WHAT DOES HE
REALLY WANT?"

"AND THE BIGGEST
QUESTION:

"WHERE
IS REX?"

89

GOOD-BYE AGAIN, MR. CHUFTAN.

MY MOST EXCELLENT FRIEND RENATA HAS CHOSEN A PATH THAT WILL ONLY LEAD TO INSECURITY, CALUMNY, AND BLOODY CARNAGE.

HER OFFSPRING HAS COME TO KNOW WHAT IT MEANS TO BE SYNTHETIC YET ALIVE!

YOU'RE SURE YOU CAN CONTROL HIM? HE SEEMS TO BE IN TOTAL CONTROL OF HIMSELF DOING WHO-KNOWS-WHAT IN THAT LAB FOR HOURS.

SNORT!

MAYBE YOU COULD JOLT HIM A COUPLE OF TIMES, JUST TO SHOW HIM WHO'S BOSS!

HE MODIFIED THE META-POLYGLYTE TO BLOCK OUTSIDE INTERFERENCE, AND LOCKED ME OUT OF THE LAB!

I APPRECIATE THAT YOU GOT ME OUT OF THAT ASYLUM AND FIXED UP MY OLD EYE, BUT YOU NEED TO GUARANTEE THAT THE MOOK WILL CARRY OUT OUR PLAN.

REX WILL BE THERE TONIGHT AT THE BLANC MASQUE AS WELL, MAMBO.

HE'LL CREATE THE DIVERSION YOU AND I WILL NEED.

TÍAS/TEE-AHS: AUNTS   QUÉ GUAPO/KAY GWAH-PO: HOW HANDSOME

MIJO/MEE-HO: MY CHILD (SHORT FOR "MI HIJO")
TÍO/TEE-OH: UNCLE

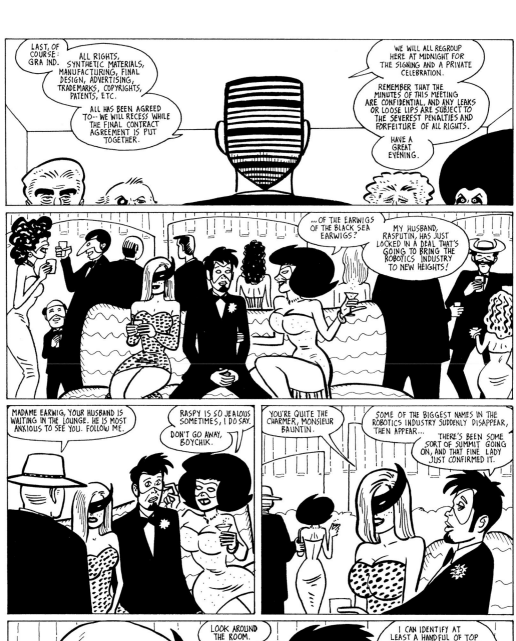

LAS TRES CHICAS QUE BAILAN EL TWIST: THE THREE GIRLS WHO DANCE THE TWIST

SORRY ABOUT YOUR "FLOPPY"-BOT BROTHER, BUT HE SERVED HIS FUNCTION VALIANTLY.

NOW, STEADY-- YOU WON'T FEEL A THING.

THERE. WE'RE IN BUSINESS.

12 AM

INSIDE THE VAN!

I THINK IT'S TIME WE TAKE OUT REX BEFORE HE GETS NEAR ANY INNOCENT BYSTANDERS.

I AGREE.

THE CHIP DEVICE IS IN PLACE, READY TO AVENGE SUSIE'S DEATH.

BYE-BYE, REX.

THAT'S THE VAN!

THE BUM TECH BOYS MEANT THAT FOR ME, BUT IT BACKFIRED ON THEM! OR DID THEY DO IT PURPOSELY SO I'D GET THE BLAME?

THANKS FOR YOUR HELP EITHER WAY, BOYS.

DULL BUSINESS ROOM...

OH, MY GOD!

NOW I REMEMBER HOW I LOST MY SHOES! GROAN!

THE 3 O'CLOCK BY BLOGGO:

A FRIEND FOR MANY YEARS...

"EVENTS HAVE A LIFE OF THEIR OWN WHEN EXPERIENCED OUTSIDE THE CONSCIOUS MIND.

"MY OWN MUDDLED MEMORIES OF AN INFAMOUS NIGHT IN QUESTION HAD ME BLISSFULLY UNAWARE OF THE DARK, DASTARDLY MIDNIGHT MACHINATIONS AND MATUTINAL LOW JINKS OF THE MOST DISTURBING KIND. AS THE NIGHTS BITE··

"THE DAYS BITE BACK.

CAMERA 1

"REX'S BIG BROADCAST OF SEVERAL WEEKS AGO, AS YOU KNOW, HAS BROUGHT A BLIZZARD OF INVESTIGATIONS, PROTESTS, RAIDS, AND GENERAL RENDING OF GARMENTS.

"THE CAPITAL GOVERNMENT HAS GOTTEN INVOLVED, AND WE MAY SEE SOME HEADS ROLL."

WE'RE DOING SOMETHING A BIT DIFFERENT THIS NIGHT!

WE'RE STARTING WITH OUR SUPER-SECRET CELEBRITY GUEST!

"STRANGER STILL IS THE FACT THAT BLOOD RELATIONS AND GOOD FRIENDS WERE IN ON THIS WHOLE DEAL UNDER MY VERY NOSE."

SO LET'S GO ON WITH THE SHOW!

OUR GUEST, A SYNTHETIC, RECENTLY A HERO IN THE TRUEST SENSE!

INTELLIGENCE, STRENGTH, HONESTY, AND A TRUE SENSE OF PURPOSE.

LADIES AND GENTLEMEN, I GIVE YOU··

HZ-
LL35!

HAZELLLLL!

"IT STANDS TO REASON THAT HAZEL WOULD GET THE SPOTLIGHT-- AFTER ALL, SHE WAS THERE FOR MOST OF IT.

"HER MEMORIES, ALONG WITH MY FAMILY'S NARRATIVE, FILLED IN SOME BLANKS I WOULD SOON REGRET HEARING.

2

"MY UNCLE TICO, KNOWN AS TIN MAN TO HIS CRONIES, WAS ON THE OUTS WITH MY GRANDMOTHER BECAUSE OF HIS TIES TO THE UNDERWORLD. HE HAD APPROACHED MY DAD WITH A DEAL TO BE A SILENT PARTNER WITH BOSS BANGAREE TO GET IN ON THE RELATIVELY NEW SYNTHETIC SKIN AND PROSTHETICS BUSINESS.

"BANGAREE BROUGHT REX OUT TO THE BIG LIFE. FATHER WAS SO IMPRESSED BY REX THAT HE PUT UP THE BULK OF THE CAPITAL FOR THE PARTNERSHIP.

"REX SEEMED TO CHARM JUST ABOUT, WELL, EVERYONE, ESPECIALLY THE NEXT GUEST."

WE INTERRUPT PROGRAMMING TO TAKE YOU LIVE TO THE 13TH DISTRICT, WHERE THE MYSTERIOUS "BLOCK" IS LOCATED.

THE MYSTERIOUS BLOCK THAT APPEARED AT THIS SPOT MONTHS AGO IS NOW BEING PREPARED TO REVEAL ITS SECRET IN A "SECRET" CEREMONY TOMORROW, ACCORDING TO POSTERS SPREAD ABOUT THE AREA.

CITY LEADERS ARE BEING VERY SECRETIVE AS TO WHAT THE BLOCK IS, OR WHAT IT MAY REPRESENT.

SEE THE BLOCK REVEALED!!

THE MYSTERY OF THE

SPECULATION IS HIGH THAT IT IS AN ART PIECE OR MONUMENT OF SOME KIND--SECURITY IS HIGH DUE TO THE FACT THAT CTZ-RX-1, A.K.A. "REX," IS STILL AT LARGE.

HE HAS BEEN SEEN FREQUENTING THIS AREA, AND IS BELIEVED ABLE TO ACTUALLY GET INSIDE THE BLOCK FROM UNDERNEATH, CAUSING VANDALISM THAT ALLEGEDLY LED TO A CONFEDERATE'S DEATH.

AND··OH! A SMALL CROWD OF WHAT LOOKS LIKE·· TAGGERS HAVE BROKEN THROUGH THE CORDON TO TRY AND TAG GRAFFITI ONTO THE BLOCK! THEY ARE BEING THWARTED BY THE BARRIER RING.

AT THE BASE OF THE BLOCK, A SQUAD OF SECURITY TROOPS GUARD THE TUNNEL ENTRANCE, AS WORKERS PUT THE FINISHING TOUCHES UP INSIDE.

EVERYTHING CHECKS OUT HERE. SHOOT-TO-KILL ORDER IS STILL IN EFFECT FOR THE PERP REX.

EXTREME PREJ. RRRROGER THAT!

OUT!

UP INSIDE THE BLOCK, A WORK CREW TAPES UP AN ELABORATE FRAMEWORK OF FIBER-OPTIC WIRES AND MINI-CAMERA DISCS IN PREPARATION FOR THE PENDING CELEBRATION!

OK, PEOPLE-- THAT'S IT.

MAKE SURE YOU STAY IN YOUR SUIT UNTIL YOU REACH THE SEALED TRANSPORT.

JUST THE GAS IN THIS PLACE WILL PEEL YOUR FACE OFF.

FROM BELOW, AS THE WORKERS EXIT THE BLOCK:

CAPTAIN, WE HAVE AN INTRUDER HEADING STRAIGHT FOR US.

I COUNT SEVEN FROM THE NORTH.

NO PRISONERS, GENTLEMEN!

HAVE THE LAUNCHER AT THE READY FOR BACKUP!

HIT 'EM WITH THE LIGHTS!

BLOGGO: "AS MY TÍAS WERE DOING THEIR 'SPINE-BREAKING' TWIST-ORNADO' DANCE DEMONSTRATION, HAZEL TOOK ME ASIDE BEFORE WE WERE TO BE PRESENTED TOGETHER."

MR. B., THERE IS SOMETHING YOU SHOULD KNOW BEFORE WE GO ON WITH THE PRESENTATION.

"IF THERE WAS EVER SUCH A THING AS TOO MUCH INFORMATION, THIS WAS IT.

"EVEN WITH HAZEL'S DIPLOMATIC APPROACH AND CHOICE OF WORDS, I WAS FREAKING OUT!

"I WAS SO OUT OF IT, I DON'T REMEMBER GOING ONTO THE SET.

"NOW MY TÍAS WERE PERFORMING A PUPPET-THEATER VERSION OF THE EVENTS OF THE TOXIC WASTE DISASTER AT THE GRA INDUSTRIES CAMPUS, LAS CACHETES, MEXICO.

"THEN MAAX PICKED UP THE STORY!"

BUILDINGS ON THE ENTIRE STREET LITERALLY MELTED TO THE GROUND. GRA SECURITY MADE SURE THE NEARBY RESIDENTS STAYED IN THEIR HOMES AND OFF THE STREETS.

THEN THE SECOND EXPLOSION WIPED OUT THE EASTERN HALF OF THE--

TÍAS: AUNTS

113

BLOGGO: "I COULD SEE THE STUDIO EXECS TRYING TO GET INTO THE CONTROL ROOM TO STOP THE BROADCAST.

"GOOD OLD MAAX-- I ALWAYS KNEW HE'D DO THE RIGHT THING SOMEDAY."

MAAX: "I WAS WORKING ON THAT BIG GRAFFITI-GOLD-MINING THING NEAR THE GRA FACILITY.

"REX SHOWS UP ON THE SITE WITH BANGAREE AND HIS LADY! SO REX TAKES OVER ON ONE END OF THE PROJECT--THE GUY IS UNBELIEVABLE!

"IT WAS...ORGANIC, MAN.

"WE CELEBRATED THE COMPLETION OF THE PROJECT AND STAYED UP TRIPPIN' FOR 3 DAYS, TALKING ABOUT NOTHING BUT PYRAMIDS AND OBELISKS...KS...KS..."

THEN THE SKY TURNED GREEN AND PURPLE.

WE WOKE UP HERE IN THE HOSPITAL AND WERE TOLD THERE HAD BEEN A FREAK FLASH FLOOD THAT TORE UP THE VALLEY, AND THAT WE WERE LUCKY TO BE ALIVE.

BLOGGO: "HAZEL AND I SAT ON THE SET AND RELATED OUR PART: HOW WE WENT TO MEXICO, ON MY TÍAS' TIP, TO GET THE STORY OF THE DISASTER THAT GRA INDUSTRIES AND THE GOVERNMENT TRIED TO KEEP QUIET."

YOU HAD BEEN DATING THE MEXICAN AMBASSADOR'S DAUGHTER, SIR. THE ART PHOTOS YOU HAD ME TAKE OF HER ARE STILL IN THE ARCHIVES. SHE HAD ARRANGED FOR US TO VISIT THE DISASTER SITE, BUT YOU NEVER LEFT THE HOTEL, REMEMBER?

HA HA HA HA HAA!

"THE LAUGH GAVE ME TIME TO COMPOSE MYSELF FOR THE REST OF IT. WHEW!"

"THEN HAZEL TALKED ABOUT HOW SHE'D GONE TO THE SITE AND ENCOUNTERED A LONE SCIENTIST DOING HER OWN RESEARCH.

"I MADE ZAZIE'S ACQUAINTANCE AND SPENT THE NEXT COUPLE OF WEEKS IN HER COMPANY WHILE I WORKED ON THE STORY. THE REST WAS A BLUR OF BREAKING THE STORY AND CELEBRATIONS AND THE APPEARANCE OF THE BLOCK..."

NEWS 5

"AND MY BLACKOUT AFTER FINDING OUT THAT I'D BEEN EXPERIMENTED ON. ZAZIE HAD REPLACED MY FEET WITH TWO EXPERIMENTAL MODELS--SO NATURALLY I FLIPPED OUT, WRECKED THE CAR, AND ACCIDENTALLY BEHEADED HAZEL! THEN, I...I...WHERE AM I...?"

MY FEET...HAZEL'S HEAD...MY SHOES...?

OH...I'M HERE, NOT...

THE TV SHOW INTERVIEW WAS A DREAM...

OH, WELL...

ZZZ...

BACK IN THE REAL WORLD: TRUTH TAKER HQ, EXPERIMENTAL WING.

THAT SHOULD BE ENOUGH. HE SEEMS TO BE OUT OF DISTRESS. HE WILL SUFFER NO ILL EFFECTS FROM THE DRUG I GAVE HIM.

Z

I AGREE. THANK YOU FOR DOING THIS, BROTHER.

THIS CITIZEN HELPED EXPOSE A GREAT WRONG DONE TO ROBOT AND HUMAN ALIKE, SO I SHALL GRANT HIM A FINAL INTERVIEW.

I AM INSTALLING THIS TINY TWO-WAY COMMUNICATOR IN HIS EAR, SO THAT I MAY INSTRUCT HIM AS TO WHEN AND WHERE.

MAY YOU HAVE PEACE THE REST OF YOUR DAYS.

THAT WAS DEFINITELY NOT THE REAL REX.

MERELY A DECOY ROBOT THAT REX CONTROLS BY REMOTE.

AND HE HAS MORE SCATTERED THROUGHOUT THE CITY, TAKING CARE OF WHAT HE CALLS "THE UNFINISHED BUSINESS OF JUSTICE," ACCORDING TO THE WHISPERS IN MY EAR.

HAZEL, WE GOTTA MOVE IF WE'RE GOING TO GET OUR INTERVIEW.

REMEMBER, HE SAID "FINAL."

117

NOW YOUR EXCELLENT FRIEND SIGI SKINK AND HER MOTHER RENATA ARE SAFE, SERGIO.

ON TO THE NEXT PHASE.

ONE OF MY DECOYS IS INFILTRATING THE CLUB AS WE SPEAK. YOU CAN WATCH THE PROCEEDINGS ON HZ-LL 35'S VIEWING HELMET. WAIT FOR THE DECOY TO BRING YOU THE VISUAL ENHANCEMENT DEVICE. YOU'LL NEED IT.

WAIT A MINUTE-- IS THIS DANGEROUS?

MAMBO ARRIVES AT HIS OFFICE THROUGH HIS SECRET ENTRANCE, AND THE CONSPICUOUS ABSENCE OF THE CUSTOMARY DRINK THAT USUALLY SITS ON HIS DESK IS NOTED.

ALL RIGHT, MOOK.

LET'S MAMBO!

MAMBO TRANCE, IT IS TIME TO PAY FOR WHAT YOU DID TO MY EXCELLENT FRIEND TANGO BANGAREE!

121

MIJO: MI HIJO: MY CHILD

IN A FEW MINUTES, THE OUTER SHELL WILL MELT AWAY TO BE ABSORBED BY THE COILED RING OUTSIDE.

THEN, A THOUSAND GALLONS OF TOXIC POLYGLYTE WASTE WILL FILL THESE CHAMBERS, TO SERVE AS A MEMORIAL FOUNTAIN IN TRIBUTE TO THOSE ROBOTS AND HUMANS ALIKE WHO SACRIFICED ALL IN THE NAME OF SCIENCE.

OUTSIDE, HIDDEN SPEAKERS START A PRERECORDED SPEECH BY THE MAYOR. THE COILED RING ACTIVATES.

-- THE BRAVE SCIENTISTS AND INNOCENTS WHO LOST THEIR LIVES IN THE TRAGEDY AT LAS CACHETES, MEXICO.

--EACH GALLON REPRESENTING THE THOUSAND SOULS, GONE TO GLORY...

THE 3 O'CLOCK, BY BLOGGO:

"*I* WENT BACK THE NEXT DAY AND THE DAY AFTER THAT. AS BEFORE, THE CAR WAS STILL THERE.

"*THE* NEW WHATEVER-IT-IS ALWAYS LOOKS DIFFERENT, DEPENDING ON THE TIME OF DAY OR NIGHT.

"*BUT* ONE MESSAGE STAYS FAITHFUL TO REX'S MEMORY. "

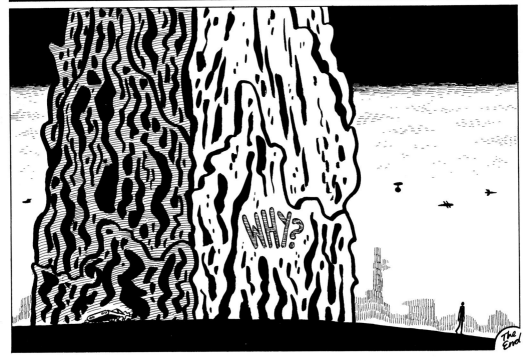

WHY?

The End

"It's 3 A.M. in the south civic plaza, and tonight I've been spit on, hit on the back with a bottle..." etcetera, etcetera.

I wrote those words a good twenty years ago scrawled on sketch paper, coming across them now and again when searching through the idea piles.

But why a toxic waste fountain?

Cut to: a vacation in Spain some years ago. While touring one of Barcelona's finer museums—the incredible Joan Miró museum, El Fundació Miró—we came across Alexander Calder's mercury fountain. Designed especially for the 1937 World's Fair in Paris, it presided with Picasso's *Guernica* in the entry hall of the Spanish pavilion.

The fountain uses actual mercury (behind really thick glass). It is also a political statement, protesting Franco's siege of the Almadén mercury mines.

The perfect symbol combining politics, the arts, and technology, as a reminder of our good intentions and our follies.

—Mario Hernandez

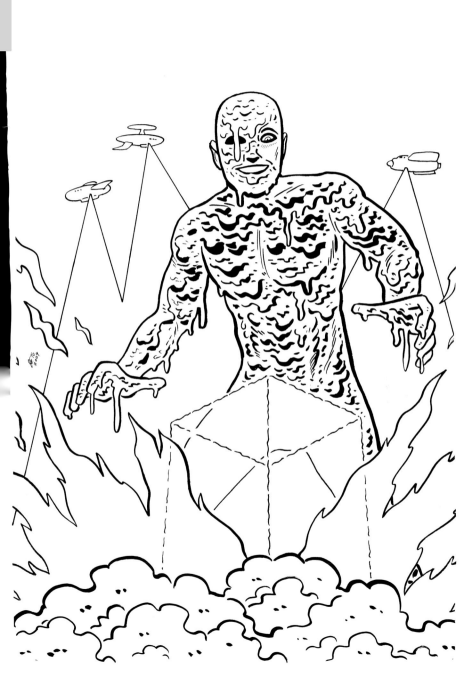

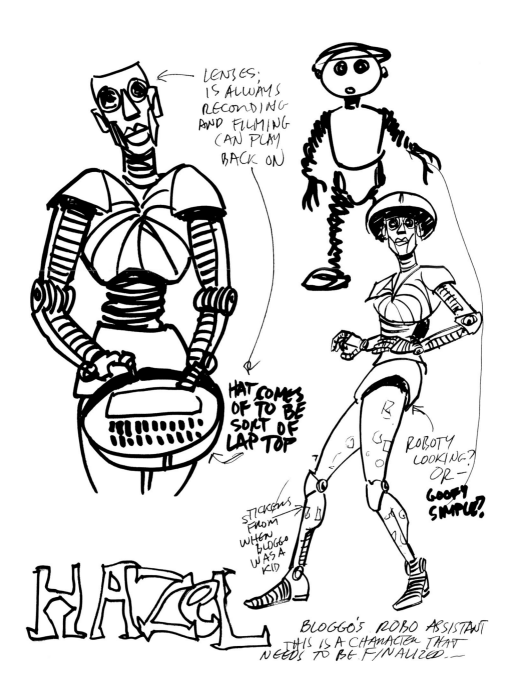

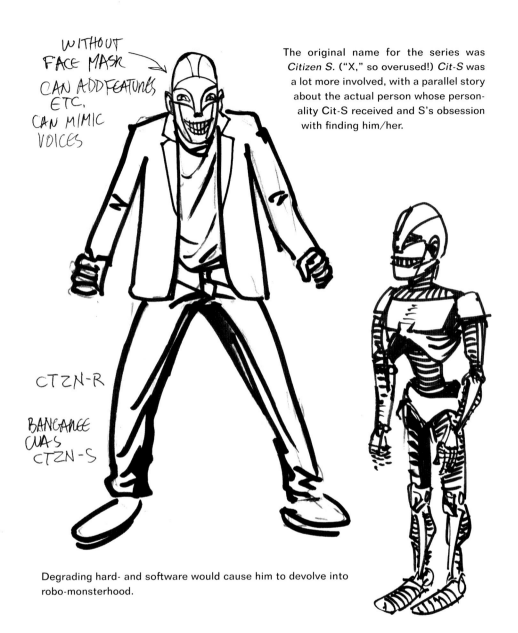

WITHOUT FACE MASK
CAN ADD FEATURES ETC,
CAN MIMIC VOICES

The original name for the series was *Citizen S.* ("X," so overused!) *Cit-S* was a lot more involved, with a parallel story about the actual person whose personality Cit-S received and S's obsession with finding him/her.

CTZN-R

BANGAMEE WAS CTZN-S

Degrading hard- and software would cause him to devolve into robo-monsterhood.

WAS INVENTED/CREATED BY BIO-LAB ALONG WITH A SECOND ONE (THAT WE FIND OUT IN A LATER ISSUE IS BANGAMEE) TO BE THE NEWEST ROBOT TO REPLACE THE CLUNKY ONES ALREADY AROUND.

COMPLETE WITH SYNTHETIC FLESH MASK AND COVERING WAS A BEAUTIFUL ROBOT BUT AFTER SOME SCANDALS WAS SHUT DOWN... DR. ZAZIE REVIVES HIM TO FIND SECOND UNIT

I pictured James Franco as Bloggo and a very young Linda Hunt as Zazie. Bloggo was to become "WEM-boy" to the gang of dogpilers hired by Zazie to find S. There was a lot more matching of wits between Bloggo, S, and Zazie—and much more of Zazie behaving badly.

"WEM" MEANS, "WATER, ELECTRICITY, MEAT" →DEROGATORY TERM FOR "WEMBOY" → NON-ROBOT = HUMAN

BLOGGO!

TRUST FUND "REBEL" KID, STARTED WRITING A RUMOR DE-BUNKING COLUMN FOR FUN, HAS BECOME A BIG MAKE OR BREAK INFLUENCE IN THE CITY - MOVES IN HIGH SOCIAL CIRCLES - IN ON THE LATEST SCANDALS

MEDICAL GENIUS
CLUELESS ABOUT
MESSING PEOPLE UP
BAD SOCIAL SKILLS

IS "SLIGHT FIGURE"
IN SCRIPT WITH
MEAT CLEAVER...

OVEN DOES
MAKE UP

LATE 50's OLD (?)
CLEAN EYES (?) NAH!
A LOT OF HAIR
5 FT. 1 INCHES
SORT OF A MORE
MANIC TINY
CONTRERAS

DOKTOR ZAZIE

BOSS BANGAREE

HEAD OF A CRIME SYNDICATE THAT IS INVESTING IN NEW MATERIALS FOR PROSTHETIC LIMBS AND DEVICES. READY TO STEAL FORMULAS AND SUCH... HIRES DR. ZAZIE

WEIRD TURBAN LIKE HAT

I SWIPED THIS WHITE OUTFIT FROM A SKA/CUBAN GROUP CALLED "SKA CUBANO" THE LEAD SINGER BENNY BILLIE DRESSES LIKE A WEIRD DIPLOMAT

Bangaree had much more screen time and more cool outfits, to be sure.

MAYBE SLICKED BACK

BRACCO, BAUNTIN

BLOGGO's DAD

Bracco Bauntin was originally a Shaman, as were his sisters.

Rex cover #2 was based on the famous Chinese political posters prevalent during and after Mao's reign, with their far-reaching messages and comment/criticism of current events.

Citizen Rex cover #4 was based on a news event
from the '70s that Gilbert told me about: a natural
disaster in Brazil sent thousands of people into the
streets, so jammed together that a man was running
on top of the crowd, filching watches, jewelry, etc.,
as he went.

Rex #3's cover came out exactly as I had pictured it
twenty years ago, when it was to be a graphic novel.

The first few issues were more tightly laid out and crammed with info. Gilbert, in his infinite wisdom, calmed them down for more breathing space.

This was the first picture of Rex that inspired the present version. As you can see by my notes, I wanted a Chester Gould feel to the story, more violent—more "Gorn," if you will. Rex would taunt the powers-that-be by sitting in plain sight inside the toxic fountain, which only he knew how to enter and exit.

Above, a sketch of Rex's helmet that he would use in order to hide whatever new face he was wearing. An homage to Kirby's original Iron Man.

CITIZEN"S" A ROBOT THAT WAS THE "STUNTBOT" FOR HAN ARTIST WHO CREATED A TOXIC FOUNTAIN ENCLOSED IN INPENETRABLE RESIN. THE ROBOT SAW THE ARTIST BETRAYED AND USED BY ART PATRONS AND POLITICIANS. HE TAKES REVENGE BY GOING AROUND BASICALLY POISONING AND USING HIS DETERIORATING SANDPAPER TYPE BODY AND SKINNING MANY ALIVE... HE TAKES THEIR CLOTHES, WEARING LAYERS THAT SHRED FROM THE CHEMICALS AND HIS SKIN.

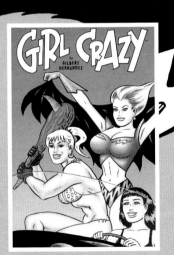
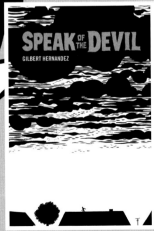